Archaeology and St

DEBATES IN ARCHAEOLOGY

Series editor: Richard Hodges

Archaeology and State Theory

Subjects and Objects of Power

Bruce Routledge

Bloomsbury Academic
An imprint of Bloomsbury Publishing Plc

B L O O M S B U R Y
NEW YORK • LONDON • NEW DELHI • SYDNEY

Bloomsbury Academic

An imprint of Bloomsbury Publishing Plc

50 Bedford Square	1385 Broadway
London	New York
WC1B 3DP	NY 10018
UK	USA

www.bloomsbury.com

**BLOOMSBURY and the Diana logo are trademarks of Bloomsbury
Publishing Plc**

First published 2014
Paperback edition first published 2015

© 2014 Bruce Routledge

Bruce Routledge has asserted his right under the Copyright, Designs and Patents
Act, 1988, to be identified as Author of this work.

All rights reserved. No part of this publication may be reproduced or
transmitted in any form or by any means, electronic or mechanical, including
photocopying, recording, or any information storage or retrieval system, without
prior permission in writing from the publishers.

No responsibility for loss caused to any individual or organization acting on
or refraining from action as a result of the material in this publication can be
accepted by Bloomsbury or the author.

British Library Cataloguing-in-Publication Data
A catalogue record for this book is available from the British Library.

ISBN: HB: 978-0-71563-633-6
PB: 978-1-4742-3713-0
ePDF: 978-1-47250-410-4
ePUB: 978-1-47250-409-8

Library of Congress Cataloging-in-Publication Data
A catalog record for this book is available from the Library of Congress.

Typeset by Fakenham Prepress Solutions, Fakenham, Norfolk NR21 8NN
Printed and bound in Great Britain

Contents

List of figures

Abbreviations

AA   *American Anthropologist*

AD   *Archaeological Dialogues*

APAAA   *Archeological Papers of the American Anthropological Association*

ARA   *Annual Review of Anthropology*

CA   *Current Anthropology*

CAJ   *Cambridge Archaeological Journal*

CQ   *Classical Quarterly*

CSSH   *Comparative Studies in Society and History*

ETCSL   *Electronic Text Corpus of Sumerian Literature* (http://etcsl.orinst.ox.ac.uk/)

JAA   *Journal of Anthropological Archaeology*

JNES   *Journal of Near Eastern Studies*

LAA   *Latin American Antiquity*

SEH   *Social Evolution and History*

Orientations

We cannot speak of the State-thing as if it was a being developing on the basis of itself and imposing itself on individuals as if by a spontaneous, automatic mechanism. The State is a practice. The State is inseparable from the set of practices by which the State actually became a way of governing, a way of doing things, and a way of relating to government.

Michel Foucault (2007: 276–7)

Today, most of us live in large-scale political communities that are at once real and unreal. Their reality is the reality of our daily experience; serving as the subject of our conversations and the object of our frustrations. Yet, these polities are also unreal in that they have no distinct material existence. We understand them to be more than just the sum of all of us, yet whenever we look closely at government itself we find only other human beings getting on with their jobs (more or less). As government, and more particularly as the state, these collectives would appear to have very real material effects that could not be executed by individuals as individuals – war, taxation, legal adjudication and enforcement, infrastructure, social services, mass education, etc. Yet, the relationship between this collective agency and other nodes of association and social power – kinship, religion, class, ethnicity, gender, market forces – is uncertain, shifting in intimacy between contexts and issues. Despite the uncertainty, we build lives on the traces left by this collective agency, such as the residency permit in my passport that prevents me from being deported. In this way we are both dominated and enabled, directed and facilitated, all without the immediate human engagement we would otherwise anticipate from persistent relationships of funda-mental importance to our lives. This collective political experience of virtual causes with material effects is familiar, interesting and conceptually difficult. In other words, it is something worth thinking about.

Many aspects of this collective political experience seem profoundly modern, but not all. Certainly war and taxation were not invented in the eighteenth century, nor, for that matter, was the experience of being 'administered'. Named polities in the past have served as the context and justification for the concentration of populations, the extraction of resources, the application of force, the execution of collective projects, and even the re-imagining of the cosmos. At the same time, we can also recognise that not all human beings have lived in such large-scale communities, and indeed for most of human history no one did. Hence, as has long been noted, there is a viable archaeological perspective on how and why such political communities exist. However, these questions present a special problem for archaeologists and ancient historians. This is not because we study the wrong side of a magic line separating modern from premodern worlds. We are, however, on the 'wrong side' of historical and disciplinary divides that render problematic the study and conceptualisation of large-scale politics in the more distant past.

Since at least the eighteenth century, political theory has usually addressed collective politics, complex polities and large-scale political domination under the more succinct, and mysterious, category of the state. Indeed, abstract reflection on the category of the state is sufficiently developed that in recent convention the phrase 'state theory' has come to refer specifically to this tradition of Western political thought (e.g. Marinetto 2007). For archaeologists, however, the state as a category presents several serious difficulties.

First is the problem of definition. Any archaeologist who has actually followed Kent Flannery's (1998: 14) directive and sought out definitions of the state in social anthropology and political science rather than archaeology is likely to have been dismayed by the result. Even within state theory the state is a vexed term, definitions of which decline in utility as they increase in precision. No one seems certain as to whether the state is a set of institutions or a kind of society, a structure of governance or a structure of coercion, a social contract or an instrument of class dominance. To define the state narrowly, say in terms of the formal offices and institutions of government, is to ignore the socially embedded nature of state power. To define the state broadly, say as a kind of encompassing social system, is to ignore the real limits of state power.

As Jens Bartelson (2001: 10–11) notes, the definition of the state is not only ambiguous, it is this ambiguity that allows the state to play a central role in political discourse. This centrality, in turn, means that the state both gathers meanings to itself and ascribes them to other terms (see Bartelson 2001: 11). Hence, words like sovereignty, authority, legitimacy, territory or civil society, words that might play a role in constructing or limiting a definition of the state, are themselves partially dependent on the category of the state for their own meanings. This is because the category of the state has been used both to describe and to shape collective politics over the past several centuries. Talking about the state helped to bring it about, and continues to help reproduce it today. This active role for state discourse presents archaeologists with their second problem, namely what to do in its absence. In other words, can one speak of the state in contexts where no historical actors were doing so themselves?

Finally, archaeologists face the special problem of their own disciplinary history. For much of the past 30 years the state in archaeological discourse has suffered from an extended neo-evolutionary hangover. For many, the very term state is synonymous with neo-evolutionism to the extent that archaeologists either wilfully avoid its serious discussion, or dissipate their energies flogging, resuscitating or genetically modifying a long-dead neo-evolutionist horse. Getting beyond this impasse requires thinking about where we are after the critique of neo-evolutionism. If the state is not what neo-evolutionists said it was, then what is it? Is it possible for archaeologists to disembed the state from social evolutionary trajectories? If so, what do we make of differences in social inequality, hierarchy, scale and centralisation across space and time? Can human political organisation be studied comparatively and what are the political implications of engaging (or not engaging) with such a project in relation to the state? In the end, is such a project even worthwhile? Why not make a clean break and bury the state along with all those other totalising concepts (e.g. race, nation, culture) that serve to create what they purport to describe?

Such questions reflect an emerging recognition that archaeologists need to think again about politics writ large. In the early days of post-processual archaeology a good start was made on thinking critically about the problem of large-scale politics from an archaeological perspective. However, the anti-essentialist basis of this critique presented an immediate problem. How could one address large-scale politics in the past without reifying the very concepts (e.g. the state) one was deconstructing in the present?

At least two solutions to this problem have been proffered in the subsequent work of archaeologists over the past 30 years. One group, often citing Michel Foucault, stated quite simply that one could not construct characterisations of large-scale politics in the past that were both critical and comparative, since critical inquiry hinged on the refusal of all such 'total' characterisations of social life (Tilley 1990: 325–8). Instead, many post-processual archaeologists pursued a strategy of turning inwards to the immediacy of their own experiences, their own bodies, and their own senses as a foundation for social and political analysis (for critical reviews see Barrett and Ko 2009; Brück 2005). In an age of torture and terror, of economic and environmental crises, this inward retreat (much like George Orwell's 'life inside the whale') seems limited, even quaint. Interestingly, it is also not the strategy that Foucault himself pursued. In refusing to begin from global categories, such as Nietzsche's 'cold monster' of the state (Foucault 2007: 109), Foucault relentlessly pursued a path to global realities by other means (e.g. Foucault 2007; 2008: 76–8, 185–8). Most particularly, these means were the specific and situated practices of power; the actual acts, localities and dispositions by which power was distributed and amplified.

In this sense, the second answer to the problem of how to critically engage with large-scale politics in the past is in fact closer to Foucault, albeit more muddled in its self-understanding. Over the past 30 years we have seen a proliferation of archaeological studies that appear to leave the category of the state largely unquestioned, even as they pursue detailed studies of particular practices (e.g. craft production, feasting, public spectacle, fiscal policies, monument construction, etc.) that served to constitute specific states (as noted already in Stein 1998: 3–5). One can characterise this trend as a shift in concern from what the state was to what a state does; that is to say a shift from a concern for entities with characteristics towards a concern for practices with effects. Despite its implicit nature, this trend represents a profound change in the conceptualisation of large-scale politics within archaeology. By focusing on the material practices that constitute particular states, archaeologists have ceased to treat the state as a singular 'thing' whose existence and form is given in the mechanism of adaptation, and have begun to address politics as a social process.

Essentially, this book is about mapping this second trend in archaeological analysis, making it explicit and giving it a little push in certain directions with potential for fruitful archaeological research. In keeping with Thomas Lemke's succinct summation of Foucault's analytics of government, I want to emphasise 'practices instead of object, strategies instead of function, and technologies instead of institution' (Lemke 2007: 58). At the same time, I want this concern for what specific human beings do to lead us back to the material presence and global effects of large-scale political domination.

I would hope that such research might be rigorous and productive, but also that it might prove relevant to politics in the broadest sense of thinking and acting collectively in the world.

While it may be idiosyncratic, this book is not radically new. I pick up and develop ideas already in circulation (see Smith 2011), including those that I myself have published elsewhere in a rather different form (Routledge 2004). What this book does provide is a brief and relatively accessible point of entry into what can be a difficult topic. In keeping with the theme of the *Debates in Archaeology* series, I have written this book as an extended argument, rather than as a general overview. It is not, therefore, a textbook in any meaningful sense. I give little attention to the history of state theory within archaeology and I focus on the development of my own arguments at the expense of judiciously representing a range of views. While I acknowledge that state-formation contributes to major social transformations at key historical junctures, I give little attention to the initial catalysts for such transformations (e.g. warfare, trade, population pressure, etc.). This is because, on one hand, many (many!) archaeologists have already addressed such catalysts in some detail, and on the other hand, a focus on initial catalysts seems to engender the attitude that a bit of hunger and warfare is all that it takes. In other words, under the right conditions states make themselves and, once made, they stay made (until they collapse, that is). In this book I want to make exactly the opposite point. Political authority is constituted by daily effort and constant cultural, social and economic production. Indeed, what we call the state has no existence save as such an on-going process. If one needs a summary of my argument in this book it is 'forget the state; focus on state-formation'.

These rather bold statements require both elaboration and justification; an endeavour that will take up much of the remainder of this book. In Chapter 1, I will specify more carefully our subject of concern, examining and modifying approaches to large-scale politics in archaeology premised on the critique of neo-evolutionism; approaches Adam Smith (2011) has recently characterised as 'archaeologies of sovereignty'. In Chapter 2 we will turn to consider why power should cohere in the forms that it does under sovereignty, giving particular attention to the problem of coercion and consent through an examination of the political writings of Antonio Gramsci. In Chapter 3 we will consider the nineteenth-century kingdom of Imerina in central Madagascar in order to illustrate Gramsci's understanding of hegemony in terms relevant to a variety of archaeological and historical contexts. In Chapter 4 we will ask how hegemonic strategies work to 'hold things together' in complex polities by articulating materially interdependent social elements and forces. In particular, the intersection of politics, gender, production and material culture will be examined in relation to both Classical Athens and the Inca Empire. In Chapter 5 we will consider more directly the practices and strategies of sovereignty along a continuum defined by the extremes of spectacle and routine. Here the practices and contexts of water management and water ritual in Classic Mayan polities will serve as a case study illuminating how spectacle and routine form two sides of a single, performative, coin. In Chapter 6 we will look at the routinised violence embedded in the funerary spectacles of the Royal Tombs of Ur as a final case study linking together the main themes of this book. Finally, our concluding chapter will reflect on the necessity, potential and problems of a comparative, politically engaged, archaeology of sovereignty.

1

After (neo-)evolution(ism)

> *... the state is neither a subject nor a thing. So how could the state act as if it were a unified subject, and what could constitute its unity as a 'thing'? And how do social actors come to act as if the state were a real subject or a simple instrument?*
>
> Bob Jessop (2007: 3)

In the epigraph hovering just above this line, Bob Jessop lays out our central problem. If states are not things, but the effects of practices, discourses and dispositions, how and why do these effects generate an apparent collective agent or instrument? In this chapter I want to explore this problem by first making it apparent and then specifying it more closely.

One place to start is with the critique of neo-evolutionism, that strand of processual archaeology where the state always seemed best loved. Vigorous critique of neo-evolutionist state theory has been on-going for at least 30 years, and indeed has increased even as its target has withered (e.g. Chapman 2003; Lull and Micó 2011; Pauketat 2007; Pluciennik 2005; Smith 2003; Yoffee 2005. For reformulations of neo-evolutionism see Marcus 2008 and Prentiss et al. 2009). If one could find a single word to characterise the central object of this critique it would probably be 'unity', or perhaps 'totality'. Despite its diversity, neo-evolutionist state theory generally presumed that societies are wholes or totalities that can conform to a limited number of social forms (*baupläne* or blueprints) defined by key traits realised across time and space. Such social forms were also presumed to resolve themselves into singular trajectories (e.g. band, tribe, chiefdom, state), determined by adaptive responses to given stimuli. For critics, this unitary view denied history, and especially the history of colonialism, by categorising contemporary tribal and peasant communities as fossilised ancestors (Fabian 1983; Pluciennik 2005). The presumed unity of state societies ignored variability in their form and institutional structure (Chapman 2003: 88–100; Pauketat 2007: 133–62), while masking class and gender distinctions (Paynter 1989; Pyburn 2004), factional competition (Brumfiel 1992) and heterarchical arrangements of power (Ehrenreich et al. 1995) that seemed to be key dynamics in actually existing states. While it is true that in the 1980s a focus on elite strategies, prestige goods and repressive power did develop (e.g. Brumfiel and Earle 1987), the 'total' nature of elite power in these models meant that the state remained unitary, if now cast as Hobbes's Leviathan rather than Hegel's divine idea. The presumption of unitary states also ignored the actual, discontinuous, spatial reality of complex polities (Smith 2003; Smith 2005). Critics have noted that political power is embedded in specific practices, buildings, settlements and landscapes, rather than abstract and homogenous territories (Smith 2003; Smith 2005). Political power is also irregularly distributed, making states more akin to networks than objects (Smith 2005).

Singular, universal trajectories, such as the necessity of chiefdoms preceding states, were criticised as empirically unsupportable in certain regions (Yoffee 1993; McIntosh 1999), not to mention teleological and ahistorical in general (Kohl 1984; Pauketat 2007). For Darwinians, this teleology showed that neo-evolutionism was not evolutionary enough (Dunnell 1980; Leonard and Jones 1987). In particular, its directional nature and its lack of a clear unit of inheritance, as well as clear mechanisms of variation and inheritance, meant that neo-evolutionism treated social evolution as something distinct from biological evolution in its processes.

The critique of neo-evolutionist state theory has opened up the state concept in archaeological analysis. In particular, it is no longer presumed to be a single package, binding together political structure, population, economic production, social differentiation and social hierarchy. It is now commonly acknowledged that polities named as states can show a considerable range of institutional arrangements (e.g. Blanton 1998), that they are characterised by internal conflict and stratagems, and dependent on the contingent social and cultural practices of specific agents (e.g. Flannery 1999). However, disassembling this package has also highlighted several unresolved conceptual problems, always latent in neo-evolutionist state theory.

Most pressing is not so much the definitional question of what the state is, as the ontological question of how states exist. While recognising that the state is not simply, or obviously, a singular entity, exactly how specific states are constituted by the practices, discourses and strategies of specific human beings remains assumed, rather than addressed, in most of the critiques of neo-evolutionism.

For example, Norman Yoffee's 'new rules' of social evolutionary theory do an admirable job of reinventing social evolution as a kind of large-scale comparative history (Yoffee 2005: 180–95). His analytical distinction between states as centralised political apparatuses and civilisations as historical configurations of elite cultural production (Yoffee 2005 17–19; Baines and Yoffee 1998; 2000) raises a number of interesting questions regarding the relationship between class, political power and cultural practices. Furthermore, Yoffee shows an acute awareness of the diversity of states, both internally in terms of the competing interests and conflicting roles they contain, and externally in terms of their institutional arrangements and social configurations. However, much as I have done in the preceding sentence, he continues to treat the state as a unified subject (e.g. states do, or have, X, Y and Z) without exploring how this subjectivity is constituted.

Similar is Robert Chapman's (2003: 95–9, 193–6; see also Lull and Micó 2011) attempt to cut the Gordian knot of the state by defining it in classic Marxist terms (e.g. Lenin 1976 [1917]) as simply the legal and coercive instrument of class dominance. Hence, for Chapman, the state arises virtually in tandem with differences in access to the means of production (e.g. ownership of land). While this approach turns our attention very directly to concrete social relations, rather than abstract taxonomies, it fails to explain just how the state is formed as an instrument and deployed as a thing (i.e. as a tool of dominant classes).

Recent applications of network analysis have, to some extent, 'fragmented' the state by modelling premodern states as networks of practices, power and resources that are concentrated in nodes linked by pathways (or 'edges' in graph theoretic terms), rather than as continuous sovereign territories (Smith 2005; Mizoguchi 2009). Yet in the end such networks remain constituent of an entity (the state) with little reflection on how this entity coheres and persists when constituted by a latticework of distinct people, places, resources and activities.

One might think that evolutionary archaeologists of a self-consciously Darwinian bent, with their intense focus on the evolution of specific cultural traits (e.g. O'Brien et al. 2010), would be well-positioned to take up the challenge of displacing the state with the analysis of practices, strategies and technologies. Yet here we encounter some interesting problems. The reproduction of any complex cultural effect, such as the state, cannot be analysed atomistically in terms of an organism or a trait. Such phenomena are inherently relational and hence dependent on the continued articulation of multiple, mutually dependent, practices (*cf.* Kuper 2000; Rosenberg 2009). Furthermore, these practices are reproduced in a niche of such intricate construction that both the proximate and ultimate causes of selection are virtually identical to specific historical sequences; essentially Yoffee's social evolution as comparative history (Yoffee 2005: 192–5). Such issues may explain the paucity of studies approaching complex polities from a 'meme's-eye view'. Indeed, the most interesting trait studies do not concern themselves with state-formation per se; rather they deploy concepts and methods derived from evolutionary biology to explore the dynamics of given traits within a framework that already presumes the state's existence (e.g. Glatz et al. 2011).

Most commonly, when state-formation is directly addressed in evolutionary terms, emphasis shifts from trait to 'group' or 'multi-level' selection. In biology, multi-level selection examines conditions under which traits that improve the reproductive fitness of a group might spread via natural selection, even when such traits decrease the reproductive fitness of specific individuals (Wilson and Sober 1994). In this view, selection can occur at any level (gene, cells, organism, population) depending upon the relationship between within-group and between-group variation and competition.

Unfortunately, when multi-level selection is applied to complex human polities, all the familiar mystifications seem to return. If groups are treated as replicators (i.e. what is being reproduced and selected) then a kind of neo-neo-evolutionism emerges, where the state as a *bauplan* for political organisation is given coherence and substance as the analogue of an organism or species (e.g. Rosenberg 2009; Spencer and Redmond 2001). When the emphasis is placed on groups as vehicles for the selection of what has been called ultrasocial human behaviour (e.g. Richerson and Boyd 2001; Turchin 2011), human groups and their organisational 'levels' are treated as already given, stable and unproblematic, rather than emergent, contextual and problematic (see Latour 2005: 27–42). Similarly, human agents are modelled as behaviourally one-dimensional and unusually consistent (e.g. altruists/prosocial versus cheaters/'free-riders'). None of this sheds much light on Jessop's problem of how and why the state becomes a non-material 'thing'.

A key issue is the lack of coherent, theoretically encompassing alternatives to the state when it comes to discussing collective politics, complex polities and large-scale political domination. For those of a post-structuralist bent this may be as it ought to be. The point of deconstruction is not to replace one reductive, totalizing framework with another, but to undermine such frameworks altogether. Hence, the appropriate heir of a totalizing concept like the state is not an alternative totality, but rather an infinite number of local possibilities.

Be that as it may, this shattering of the unitary state concept is not what has actually happened over the past 30 years. Indeed, regardless of the theoretical predilections of individual scholars, whenever archaeologists have turned their attention to large-scale political domination the state, or something very much like it, has sneaked back in.

Even scholars with impeccable post-processual credentials, engaged in projects with explicitly anti-essentialist objectives, still end up framing their studies in terms of large-scale reified polities.

Lynn Meskell (2002), in her book *Private life in New Kingdom Egypt*, must presume an entity called 'New Kingdom Egypt' in order to imagine the space that makes possible the very concept of an ancient Egyptian private life. In his book *Art and the early Greek state*, Michael Shanks (1999) addresses the concept of the state more directly, but he does so in order to hold it constant as a backdrop against which are played out figurative and literary discourses on status, sexuality, masculinity and violence. One could argue that in each of these cases the authors are not perpetuating a universal social form, but merely reproducing indigenous categories (i.e. the land of Egypt, or the Greek *polis*). Yet this in itself implies some rather interesting questions. Why has it been necessary for ancient authors, modern neo-evolutionists and post-modern critics to imagine large-scale politics in terms of reified entities that literally do not exist in any physical sense? More to the point, we might echo Jessop (2007: 3) and ask how it is that historical actors come to view such entities as if they did have a physical existence. It seems that we face something of a paradox. How do we account for the apparent coherence of large-scale political domination without returning to some kind of unitary state?

Adam Smith's (2003) approach to these problems is distinct and worth considering for the manner in which he moves decisively beyond post-structuralist refusal. Smith (2003: 84–7) follows contextualist historians (e.g. Skinner 1989) in noting that the semantic meaning of the state, as a doubly impersonal edifice distinct from both ruler and ruled, has a distinctly modern history linked to political developments in Europe since the sixteenth century. The state, therefore, is a historically specific concept presented as a natural object for political ends. Smith argues that the retroactive application of this concept to archaeological contexts provides an inadequate analytical account of past political practices. At best, it turns the analysis of actual political processes into a taxonomic exercise. At worst, projecting the state into premodern contexts extends and naturalises asymmetrical power structures in the present day. In this way archaeologists fall victim to what Pierre Bourdieu (1999: 54) describes as 'a state, which still thinks itself through those who attempt to think it …'

Like many other scholars, Smith follows his principled rejection of the state concept with the introduction of an alternative placeholder, something he terms 'Early Complex Polities' (Smith 2003: 102–5). However, the strength of Smith's argument lies in his unwillingness to leave the reification of Early Complex Polities unquestioned. Hence, while he defines such polities loosely in terms of traits that are indistinguishable from those of the 'Archaic State' (Smith 2003: 102–5) and designates them as the 'class of objects under examination' (Smith 2003: 102), he immediately shifts his attention from traits to 'the relationships that constitute the political sphere of action' (Smith 2003: 102).

For the purpose of analytical precision, Smith describes these relationships in terms of four levels, moving from the relationships between polities to the relationships between regimes, subjects and institutions. However, if we step back from Smith's organising scheme we realise something fundamentally important about the analysis of collective politics and complex polities. What is under examination is not a class of objects named Early Complex Polities, nor is it even an ensemble of distinct objects such as regimes, institutions or subjects. What Smith examines are the relations, practices and discourses that constitute these objects as effects. Taken together, these effects constitute what Smith terms political authority, and it is this constitution of political authority that he places at the heart of any analysis of politics in early complex polities (Smith 2003: 105).

For Smith, political authority is authority, meaning the effect of a 'posited, perceived, or institutionally ascribed asymmetry between speaker and audience' (Lincoln 1994: 4, as quoted in Smith 2003: 106), extended to be the authority of last resort in a given territorial context. The analysis of political authority, then, is the analysis of '… how, in varying sociocultural formations, an authoritative political apparatus came to gain varying degrees of ascendancy over all other social relations' (Smith 2003: 108).

As is well known, not all communities or societies have been structured by political relationships in which some person or institution has the 'last word' in the sense of making decisions that are authoritative and binding for all members (see Clastres 1977; Graeber 2004). Smith, therefore, continues to recognise that there are important differences in the kinds of political relationships that exist and have existed within human societies. Such differences can form the basis for meaningful comparative study and even a renewed engagement with social evolution. However, Smith's focus on political relationships, and the practices and settings through which they are constituted, also implies a shift in how archaeologists are to approach such comparative study. In particular, it turns our attention away from the supposedly inherent traits of an entity or system and towards the actual socio-spatial networks through which power is constituted (*cf.* Mann 1986: 1–18).

This said, political authority on its own does not provide all of the tools that we need to understand large-scale political domination. First, despite the centralising logic of political authority, no political apparatus ever gains 'varying degrees of ascendancy over *all* other social relations'. As Michael Mann notes, if we understand power in terms of socio-spatial networks of relationships, then these networks always contain interstices (Mann 1986: 16). Whether in the form of rebellion, criminality, token submission or the tacit recognition of domains where it is never asserted, political authority always encounters limits in its realisation (Hansen and Stepputat 2006). These limitations can be practical and technological, but they are not accidentally or exclusively so. Quite simply, the limits of political authority are inherent in the possibility of difference and of resistance.

As the literature on heterarchy reminds us, even at its centre political authority can be multi-centric, dispersed in multiple locales, or alternatively strong or weak depending on the context and issues at stake (e.g. Ehrenreich et al. 1995). What is significant about political authority is not that a political apparatus does, or does not, 'gain ascendancy over all other social relations', but rather that the promise and potential of that ascendancy is produced and reproduced despite its effective absence in specific contexts. This implies at least two things: one is that political authority needs to be imagined or represented as continuous even though it is not; the other is that political authority in the form of a political apparatus (be it one person or a set of institutions) cannot stand alone, but must be linked to other social forces, interests and orders in a complementary manner if it is to be imagined as continuous (see Chapter 4).

One way of reproducing political authority at the limits of its realisation is by means of force. Certainly, one must presume that the threat of coercive force, be it physical or symbolic (see Bourdieu 1999: 56), underlies the 'last resort' in Smith's definition of political authority. Relations of force are, of course, very much part of classic state theory. Here we find two distinct emphases. On one hand, there is a concern for force directed outwards via warfare, both as a state function (Clausewitz's 'continuation of policy by other means') and as a catalyst to state formation (historically and organisationally). In this view, to quote Charles Tilly (1975: 42), 'wars made the state and the state made wars'. On the other hand, there is a concern for force directed inwards via legislative, judicial and police powers. This is Max Weber's (1978: 54) state as a political organisation claiming a monopoly on legitimate violence within a given territory. Both sorts of relations of force stand at the limits of political authority (i.e. the point where consent falters) and are therefore interesting for the ways in which they are kept distinct. Put simply, warfare is distinguished from law and policing by structures of identity (e.g. interior/exterior; us/them) and concepts of legitimacy in the uses of violence.

Once linked to political authority, warfare is undeniably important as a means of acquiring and defending resources. It can also serve as a justification, even foundation, for authority itself (Agamben 2005). However, as collective violence enacted across communal/identity boundaries, warfare is not strictly dependent on political authority in Smith's terms. Warfare occurs between communities lacking any authority of 'last resort' (Keeley 1996). Indeed, Pierre Clastres (1977) went so far as to argue that, in the Amazon basin, continual warfare between communities was a tactic that prevented chiefs from accumulating resources and authority within communities. So, whereas Thomas Hobbes claimed that life outside the state was a 'warre of every man against every man' (Hobbes 1968 [1651]: 188), it seems that the real problem is within the state, where warfare must be distinguished from the internal deployment or threat of coercive force. As Weber recognised, this makes the question of legitimacy central to the question of political authority. So, in addition to analysing the practices and relationships that constitute political authority, we also need to give attention to the practices and relationships of coercive force (both physical and symbolic; see Bourdieu 1999) and the problems of legitimacy these entail.

Smith (2011: 416) has in fact recognised the link between political authority and coercive force in his more recent work, where he now employs the term 'sovereignty' to refer to relations of political authority grounded in violence (following Agamben 1998 and Hansen and Stepputat 2006 in generalising Foucault's understanding of premodern sovereignty – on which, see pp. 21–2). However, one final problem remains. While Smith clearly avoids the error of starting from reified entities like the state, such entities are still constituted, both abstractly in his analytical framework (e.g. Early Complex Polities) and historically in actual political formations (e.g. the kingdom of Urartu). Smith gives ample attention to the spatial practices of this reification in his discussion of polities (Smith 2003: 149–83). However, it is not clear from his conceptual framework why such reification needs to occur in the first place. Why must political authority, as the authority of last resort, be experienced and analysed in these virtual terms?

De-centring the state

A starting point is to note that the modern state is one example of political authority realised in virtual terms and that we can learn a good deal from attempts to critically analyse its virtual nature. Smith (2003: 96–7) correctly notes that in widely cited articles both Philip Abrams (1988) and Timothy Mitchell (1999) have explored 'the senses in which the state does not exist' (Abrams 1988: 82) as an entity unto itself. However, it is important to note that the arguments of each scholar go beyond the uses that Smith has made of them. Indeed, these critical strands of state theory seek to de-centre the state: not simply to note that it does not actually exist, but rather to examine how the presumption of its existence has real material effects.

Abrams (1988: 73), for example, concedes that social cohesion is one function of politics in class societies. However, he argues that if one says that this cohesive function is what the state provides, one has already assigned a misplaced concreteness to the state, thereby simplifying and mystifying actual political practice. Instead, Abrams distinguishes between the state idea and the state system. The state idea refers to a discursive construct ('the state') that:

> ... presents institutionalised power to us in a form that is at once integrated and isolated and by satisfying both these conditions it creates for our sort of society an acceptable basis for acquiescence. It gives an account of political institutions in terms of cohesion, purpose, independence, common interest and morality without necessarily telling us anything about the actual nature, meaning or functions of political institutions. (Abrams 1988: 68)

The state idea, therefore, attributes '... unity, morality and independence to the disunited, amoral and dependent workings of the practice of government' (Abrams 1988: 82). These practices of government are what Abrams refers to as the state system and they are constituted by the disparate ensemble of institutions, structures and agencies that act to ensure the continued domination of key sectional interests in modern capitalist societies. For Abrams the state idea is necessary and real because without it the interested and illegitimate nature of the domination achieved through the state system would be exposed. Hence, his widely quoted statement: 'In sum, the state is not the reality which stands behind the mask of political practice. It is itself the mask which prevents us seeing political practice as it is' (Abrams 1988: 82).

Timothy Mitchell takes up Abrams's argument, but notes that distinguishing the state idea from the state system is not as easy as Abrams implies. This is because, without the state idea, the practice of government has no distinct location, being simply the social practices of disciplinary power in general. For Mitchell, there is no point in distinguishing the real and the illusory aspects of the state, since the central question for the modern state is how and why the mundane practices of disciplinary power constitute the state idea as an abstract form; dividing state, society and economy as if these were discrete structures, agents or things. As Mitchell (1999: 77) notes: 'the phenomenon we name "the state" arises from techniques that enable mundane material practices to take on the appearance of an abstract, nonmaterial form'.

Following on from Mitchell, we can see that there is an intimate relationship between the state idea and the material practices of power in modern states. As Mitchell suggests, the state idea is constituted and given substance by repeated, and seemingly mundane, practices of regulation, monitoring, definition and enforcement. At the same time, the state idea does more than mask or justify the workings of power, as it orients and articulates the state system in the moment of practice. By orients I mean that the state idea allows people to act in the name of, or with regard to, the state. This serves to remove their actions from the realm of everyday human relations and place them in a virtual realm of relations between citizens and the state. By articulating I mean that the state idea provides the political cohesion necessary to align social interests and forces in emergent configurations. In other words, the state idea provides what Foucault (2007: 286) termed the 'principle of intelligibility' for governmental practices.

It may seem odd to turn to Foucault in discussing the idea of the state, especially in a book that is ultimately concerned with premodern contexts. Foucault was well known for his apparent disinterest in state theory, even stating: 'I do, I want to, I must do without a theory of the state, as one can and must forgo an indigestible meal' (Foucault 2008: 76–7). Furthermore, for some, Foucault's concept of 'governmentality' as a series of techniques, or arts, of government predicated on the management of populations as entities represents a radical break, both conceptually in relation to classic state theory and historically in its distinctly modern point of reference. However, the recent publication (Foucault 2007) of the wider programme of lectures within which Foucault developed his ideas on governmentality makes clear that it is incorrect to suggest (as I did in Routledge 2004: 16–17) that he did not engage with the concept of the state (see Jessop 2007: 140–54; Lemke 2007).

Foucault does argue that the modern era (especially from the late eighteenth century) is marked by the recognition of human population as something with its own mechanisms and qualities that can be facilitated and managed through practices of governance that are not limited to a central political apparatus (e.g. insurance, opinion polls, public health, etc.). However, he does not oppose this governmentality to the state; indeed, he argues that the reflexive recognition of the state as an abstract category emerges in tandem with these new arts of governing a population, serving as their principle of intelligibility (Foucault 2007: 247–8, 276–8).

Importantly for our purposes, Foucault also acknowledges that the idea of the state was 'a way of thinking the specific nature, connections, and relations of certain already given elements and institutions' (Foucault 2007: 286). In other words, these transformations in both the arts of government and their principle of intelligibility occurred within an already existing political context. Foucault, for example, acknowledges that 'the state as a set of institutions of sovereignty has existed for millennia' (Foucault 2007: 120) and that the problem of sovereignty both predates the idea of governing a population and continues alongside governmentality as a pressing concern (Foucault

2007: 106–8). For Foucault (2007: 11), sovereignty refers to the ability to command and forbid in a binding manner within a given territory. In short, it is very similar to Smith's definition of political authority. What changes between the late sixteenth and late eighteenth centuries, therefore, is the techniques through which sovereignty is constituted and manifest (population management as opposed to law and force alone) and the principles through which these techniques are made intelligible (e.g. the state and *raison d'État* as opposed to divine right and God's law). Stated throughout Foucault's lectures, but left undeveloped, is the fact that premodern political authorities and their institutions of sovereignty were also dependent on specific techniques and practices with their own principles of intelligibility.

To summarise; the modern state provides us with an example of virtual political authority because it rests on specific practices of governance that lend substance and effect to the concept of the state, even as that concept renders these practices intelligible (by providing orientation and articulation). Both the concept of the state and at least some of these practices of governance may well have been inventions of the modern era, but they were not *de novo* inventions. The modern state as a doubly impersonal edifice, at once secular and transcendent, displaced earlier constructions of political authority that were equally transcendent, if neither impersonal nor secular (e.g. the divine right of kings).

Think for a moment of the ancient Greek *polis*; while it could be represented as an abstract category, it could never be viewed as something distinct from the political community itself (i.e. it was society and hence could not govern it – see Anderson 2009 and Hansen 1998), and hence is very different from the state idea (see Chapter Four). At the same time, the imagining and experiencing of the collective will of the *polis* as a form of communal agency, one that was constituted in articulation with key social interests and forces (e.g. slavery and patriarchy), formed a kind of virtual political authority that would both match the definitions of Smith and be amenable to analysis along the lines of those proposed by Mitchell.

Admittedly, for most monarchies even this level of abstraction was rare, with explicit political theory generally replicating Louis XIV's 'l'état c'est moi'. Yet, even in the most personal forms of political authority we find a virtual element that suggests that we might learn something of general significance from the critical analysis of the modern state. Political authority in Pharaonic Egypt, for example, was quite clearly and exclusively invested in the Pharaoh. However, both the Pharaoh and his (or her) subjects were transformed in rather interesting ways by a number of material practices. Best known, of course, is the deification of the Pharaoh as the embodiment of Horus while alive and Osiris when dead. In this role, the Pharaoh was charged with maintaining *ma'at* ('right order') on earth, keeping the forces of chaos at bay (Teeter 1997). Yet, while ancient Egyptians never articulated a formal distinction between office and office-holder, it is clear that this deification was not attached to the person of the Pharaoh as an individual, but rather to his (and occasionally her) role as king (O'Connor and Silverman 1995: xxv). Indeed, a large number of material practices served to transform the nature of each Pharaoh on his (or her) ascent to the throne. The title Pharaoh (*pr '3*) itself means 'the great house' (i.e. palace), hence the king as Pharaoh was not simply an individual but embodied in himself or herself the palace and its household estate (O'Connor 1995). By the New Kingdom this title could be used in both ritual and administrative documents without reference to the name of the sitting Pharaoh, and hence could be ascribed an abstract quality, especially within scribal and artistic genres that spanned multiple centuries. Conventions for marking-off the Pharaoh's throne name, such as enclosing it in a cartouche or always following it with the phrase 'life, prosperity and health', had this same historical quality such that their repetition for successive Pharaohs over long periods of time served to assimilate each of those individuals to the broader category of Pharaoh. Indeed, even the adoption of throne names and titles itself served to mark the transformation of the heir into something other than merely human on ascension to the throne.

The subjects of the Pharaoh were also defined by material practices through which they were collectively bounded and differentiated from those that surrounded them. In contrast to the expectations of scholars such as Anthony Giddens (1985), the Egyptian state seemed to have a concept of its geographical boundaries. For example, in a recently discovered inscription from Zawiyat er-Rahman, a fort on ancient Egypt's Libyan frontier, the commander Neb-Re takes the title 'one who brings an end to the transgressors of his boundary' (Steven Snape, personal communication). As is well-known (e.g. Leahy 1995), non-Egyptians are portrayed visually via a limited number of stereotypical features (hair and beard style, clothing, skin colour) that serve to identify them with a limited set of foreign identities (e.g. Nubian, Libyan, Syrian, Hittite, etc.) and contrast them with native Egyptians. Usually, such foreigners appear as props in scenes of triumphant xenophobia (e.g. head-smitings, bound prisoners, tribute bearers). Even more subtle, however, is the visual nature of hieroglyphs, which makes it impossible to write the words for male or female human being without depicting a specifically Egyptian person (see Goldwasser 2002: 21–2).

These, and many more, material practices served to transform political authority in ancient Egypt from an asymmetrical relationship between persons (and hence subject to mutual recognition between participants) into a virtual relationship between the Pharaoh and his (or her) subjects. The virtual nature of this relationship meant that it was defined categorically and *a priori*, rather than being dependent on the nature, quality and context of the relationship between specific participants. This provided a frame of reference within which political authority was released from constraints that might otherwise limit its ability to compel. For example, one did not need to interact directly with any specific Pharaoh in order to know the power and authority of the Pharaoh. More pointedly, it would release political authority from cultural and social restrictions on the contexts in which, and degree to which, physical and symbolic coercion could be enacted. Certainly, relations of dominance, including physical violence, are frequently sanctioned between genders and ages or within kin groups in otherwise 'egalitarian' societies. However, such sanctions are made possible by their limits, that is to say by the contexts in which open coercion is denied and hence gender- or age-based identities are differentiated and differentially valued (e.g. the oxymoron of 'egalitarian' patriarchal communities). The virtual relationships of political authority are fundamentally different in this regard because they recognise no such limits on the possibility of coercion in the last instance (Agamben 1998; 2005).

Yet, even as transcendence frees authority from moral constraints on violence, it also allows that authority to be delegated, responsive and discontinuous without surrendering its claims to being centralised and monolithic. For example, although Inca rulers were ostensibly the sole leaders in war, religion and politics, in practice they included under their personal exploits the achievements of various surrogates, such as generals, the high priest of the Sun, and administrative officials called the 'Inca's substitute' (*Incap rantin*). Hence, in the words of Peter Gose, '... the Inka became a kind of umbrella figure or corporate persona, who hierarchically subsumed under his identity an entire supporting cast of lesser individuals' (Gose 1996: 17).

My description of virtual political authority shares much in common with Maurice Bloch's arguments regarding the role of ritual in constituting royal authority as transcendent in relation to everyday life (Bloch 1987: 271–4). However, I see no need to limit the constitution of such transcendence to ritual action, unless defined in its broadest sense as habitual practice. I also see no need to limit transcendence to specifically royal (i.e. personal) political authority. Certainly, the modern state is constituted as a transcendent idea (e.g. 'distinct from both ruler and ruled'), one that transforms actual relations between people into virtual relations between citizens and the state. Hence, transcendent sovereigns and sovereign states are not the same thing, but they are different manifestations of the problem highlighted by Jessop at the beginning of this chapter.

Summation

In this chapter I have argued that what we frequently call state-formation entails not the formation of an entity, but the configuring of relationships around political authority made transcendent and grounded in violence. In the remainder of this book I will follow Adam Smith (2011) and others in calling this configuration 'sovereignty', with the understanding that sovereignty entails the political effect of transcendence, as much as it does authority and violence. It remains to explore how and why sovereignty, understood in these terms, has been achieved in different times and places – a task that will occupy our attention for the remainder of this book.

2

Coercion and consent

*The pack of scoundrels tumbling through the gate, emerges as the
Order of the State.*

Stanley Kunitz, *The System* (1971)

Sovereignty is easy enough to imagine, but more difficult to imagine in
a realistic manner, one in which a master plan is not evident, in which
specific people applaud, resist or ignore specific projects, in which
necessary resources are not automatically present, and in which the
material interests of potential rulers, officials and subjects may be in
direct conflict with one another. Why should practices and strategies
cohere in this manner, often against all odds and against the material
interests of at least some of those involved?

Order, legitimacy and wealth

One innovative attempt to come to terms with such issues is John
Baines and Norman Yoffee's (1998; 2000) comparative account of the
relationship between power and culture in early Egypt and Mesopotamia.
Baines and Yoffee contend that in both of these early civilisations it is
precisely the civilisational component that must be grasped if one is
to understand the production and reproduction of political authority.
In particular, Baines and Yoffee argue that political authority in early
states is embedded in a matrix of what they refer to as 'high culture'.
They argue that in both Egypt and Mesopotamia the cultural activity
of an inner elite created dominant systems of meaning that hinged in
particular on the imagining of an encompassing cosmological order.

Order in this sense provided a single intellectual framework capable of incorporating religious, social, political and economic life. As such, it made the actions, duties and existence of kings and other elites central to the stability and continuity of the cosmos itself, in so far as they were called upon to maintain or renew order through ritual, adjudication or force. This, of course, served to legitimate specific dynasts, but it also provided definitions and criteria for legitimacy independent of individual regimes and hence available for activation beyond the temporal and/or spatial limits of any given regime. Over time, the reproduction of a common cosmological order could provide a consistent framework for reviving political authority and political centralisation despite the regular collapse of specific regimes.

For example, in the case of Pharaonic Egypt, the reproduction of 'high culture' as the matrix of political authority allowed the revival of centralised rule expressed in symbolically consistent forms after periods of political decentralisation (i.e. after the First, Second and Third Intermediate periods). Notably, it even provided a literary and visual language of authority for rulers such as the Ptolemies, who were explicitly non-Egyptian in their ethnicity. In the case of early Mesopotamia, a regional 'high culture' provided a common matrix for political authority, both between competing city-states and within city-states, where distinct temple and palace institutions were simultaneously semi-autonomous and mutually engaged in ruling and administering the city's population, resources and territory.

For early China, Kwang-chih Chang (1983: 9–33, 107) has argued that a shared ideology of clan hierarchy based on divine descent provided a mythological framework within which different clans could legitimately compete for rulership. Evidence for early centralisation in the Erlitou and Erligang phases (beginning of the Bronze Age in northern China), that stands in contrast to the later segmented and competitive political landscape of Late Shang and the remaining 'Three Dynasties' period, suggests that this segmented political landscape should perhaps be seen more historically and less structurally than Chang implies (see Liu 2009). Regardless, Baines and Yoffee's focus on

cosmological order is rather helpful in understanding the continuity
to be seen in the reproduction of political authority in Late Shang and
Zhou-period China despite the shifting fates of specific regimes and
lineages. In this context, the amassing and utilisation of wealth was a key
component in materialising, celebrating and reproducing the cosmological order. This occurred directly through temple and funerary
ritual, as well as military campaigns. It also occurred indirectly through
the production of buildings, monuments, spectacles and objects that
overwhelmed and/or enchanted the senses. Secondarily, access to, and
knowledgeable consumption of, the products of 'high culture' also
served as an identity token, forging shared experiences and a cohesive
worldview amongst the 'inner elite' of early Egypt and Mesopotamia.
Hence, economic production, as the production of wealth, was not an
end in itself that needed justification; rather it was the means to an end
(i.e. the production and reproduction of order) whose justification lay
in the perceived legitimacy of that end.

Understanding the constitution of political authority in terms of
a wider order that is not contained or produced within the limits of
a governmental apparatus is one of the more insightful aspects of
Baines and Yoffee's broad comparison of Egypt and Mesopotamia. This
allows us to understand historical continuity in the representation
of authority in spite of the rise and fall of specific regimes. It also
highlights that polity formation incorporates a cultural logic, and not
merely the adaptive logic of managerialism or the exploitative logic of
political economy. Hence, order and its legitimation are elaborated,
believed in and pursued beyond what is strictly necessary in order to
organise a population or mask exploitation.

However, as a number of commentators have pointed out (see
Richards and Van Buren 2000), Baines and Yoffee's approach is severely
limited by its strong emphasis on the exclusive and exclusionary
nature of 'high culture'. While the problem of non-elite integration
is continually raised in both of Baines and Yoffee's papers (Baines
and Yoffee 1998: 232–3, 240, 246; 2000: 15, 16–17), they repeatedly

conclude that not only is there little evidence for the participation of non-elites in the 'high culture' of Egypt and Mesopotamia, but there is also little evidence for the materialisation of any alternative ideologies (Baines and Yoffee 1998: 240). Apparently, in both early Egypt and Mesopotamia the alternative to 'high culture' was no culture. Not surprisingly, this position has been resisted by scholars otherwise sympathetic to Baines and Yoffee's approach.

Janet Richards (2000), for example, documents the development of mass cemeteries in the First Intermediate period of Egypt and the widespread distribution of amulets worn on the body that consistently replicate the symbols and signs of Egyptian 'high culture' including those from the supposedly exclusive domain of hieroglyphic writing. Richards also points to an increased emphasis on, and dispersal of, spatial (e.g. temples, processional ways) and material (e.g. stele, statues) products inviting spectatorship of, or participation in, state rituals and high cultural practices during the Middle Kingdom. This is paired with the rise of literature concerned with moral order, and the 'private' orientation of elites to this order (*cf.* Parkinson 2002). In stories such as the 'Tale of the eloquent peasant', this moral order is clearly extended to the treatment of non-elites, suggesting that such persons presented moral and ideological problems for elites that would be difficult to imagine in the strictly bifurcated terms used by Baines and Yoffee (see Routledge 2003).

Norman Yoffee's own study of law courts and conflict resolution in early Mesopotamia (Yoffee 2000), as well as work on Old Babylonian local councils by his student Andrea Seri (2005), points towards a complex accommodation of, and interrelationship with, local forms of authority on the part of central governments in early second millennium BC Mesopotamia. Again, this would seem to contrast with the rather one-sided picture of elite exclusivity painted by Baines and Yoffee's general comparative account.

More striking perhaps in its use of long-term archaeological evidence is Rowan Flad's (2008) recent study of the development of oracle bone divination in early China from the late Neolithic through the Shang and early Zhou periods. Evidence for osteo-pyromancy, so named because the bones are burned to catalyse the cracking on which divination is based, can be traced continuously from third millennium BC Longshan sites through to early first millennium BC Western Zhou sites (Flad 2008: 406–18). As is well known, during the Late Shang period (late second millennium BC) many such oracle bones (especially cattle scapulae and turtle plastrons) were carefully prepared and inscribed as part of divination rituals closely linked to Shang rulers. Divination in the Shang court was clearly an example of what Baines and Yoffee would call 'high culture', a practice involving elite specialists and closely linked to early Chinese concepts of order and legitimacy. At the same time, these inscribed oracle bones are preceded by a long history of less specialised, and widely dispersed, osteo-pyromanic practices involving uninscribed bones. Furthermore, even within Shang contexts, inscribed bones are far outnumbered by uninscribed bones and it seems unlikely that such divinatory activities were a state monopoly (see Campbell 2008; Jing 2008).

Shang osteo-pyromancy appears to be a case of what I have elsewhere termed entrainment (see Routledge 2004: 185–90). By this I mean the linking of cultural practices, with their own history and social distribution, to political authority such that the former not only serves to reproduce the latter, but is also transformed by it. This transformation can occur both in the mechanics of the cultural practice itself and in its indexical value as a sign of political authority. My original example was the use of alphabetical writing in the Iron Age Levant, whose Bronze Age invention and early Iron Age development is not effectively analysed as an exclusive product of 'high culture' or the state. At the same time, alphabetic writing does become linked to the function and representation of kingship in the course of the Iron Age, and is transformed as a result. Similarly, osteo-pyromancy has a long history in China, and both its appeal to Shang rulers and the power implicit in the specialised skill of royal Shang diviners, lay in the fact that divination was embedded, and valued, in a wider cultural context. The tension between royal co-optation and this wider cultural context for divination is perhaps acknowledged in the fourth century BC text *Kuo Yü* where it is explained that in the past everyone could communicate between earth and heaven via gifted shamans (*hsi/wu*), but this broke down when households began to perform their own religious rites and humans and spirits freely intermingled, with calamitous results. To restore order, free communication between heaven and earth had to be severed and carefully managed by the royal court (see Chang 1983: 44–5).

While embedded in long-standing cultural practices, the entrainment of osteo-pyromancy by Shang rulers resulted in developments such as the addition of inscriptions and specialised preparation of the bone surface that presumably transformed what it meant to be a skilled diviner. One need not presume, therefore, that Shang rulers had to hold a monopoly on osteo-pyromancy in order to gain power from their specialised skills in divination. Once cultural practices become marked by their association with political authority, they can serve as an indexical sign, calling to mind that authority in contexts where political authority plays no direct role as either author or authoriser.

Rational choice?

In a recent, rather monumental cross-cultural survey Richard Blanton and Lane Fargher (2008) present an argument almost directly opposed to that of Baines and Yoffee, addressing what has been called 'Hobbes's dilemma' in the context of premodern states. 'Hobbes's dilemma' is summed up in the simple question 'what holds a collective (such as a state) together given the tendency for human beings to pursue their own self-interest?' Blanton and Fargher suggest that this question cannot be answered in the uni-directional terms of elite domination. They apply rational choice theory to argue that, as rational agents, subjects in premodern states ('tax-payers' in their terminology) would have actively negotiated and agitated for the provision of key 'public goods' (e.g. security, adjudication, law enforcement, water supply, transport routes, etc.), in return for the resources they surrendered to Baines and Yoffee's 'inner elites' ('state principals' in their terminology). Such negotiated consent was necessary, as coercion alone would be too expensive and ineffective a means of ensuring 'tax-payer compliance'. Hence, according to Blanton and Fargher, collective action, as the negotiated trade-off of public revenues in return for public goods, is a variable relevant to all states, modern or premodern. Using quantitative analysis, they suggest that the degree to which a state is characterised by collective action is determined largely by the degree to which 'state principals' are dependent on extracting revenue from tax-payers rather than from other sources (e.g. war booty, trade monopolies, royal land-holding, etc.). Furthermore, Blanton and Fargher suggest that states characterised by collective action would develop more extensive, socially penetrating, bureaucracies in order to discover, address and enforce public will and the provision of public goods.

Blanton and Fargher are certainly correct in arguing that the consent of subjects plays a role in all political authority, and that this consent cannot be presumed but must be continually elicited and reproduced over time. The question is whether or not this consent is simply a matter of balancing individual interests against the common good (or a ruler's ambitions against her subjects' needs), as Blanton and Fargher seem to suggest. Notably, Blanton and Fargher accept as given several fundamental categories and relationships that, as we saw in Chapter 1, become rather problematic on closer examination.

The state as an entity and the virtual relationship of ruler to subject, with its accompanying right to both extract resources and provide public goods, are presumed rather than examined by Blanton and Fargher. For example, they do not ask why the state principals/ tax-payer relationship exists in the first place, nor how it is reproduced over time.

While the diversity of interests present in any human collective is central to 'Hobbes's dilemma', Blanton and Fargher's tax-paying subject is an undifferentiated and homogenous rational actor. Yet, certain of their key public goods, such as the enforcement of tax-payer compliance and the prevention of 'free-riding', already imply that tax-payer consent and the definition of a public good is not undifferentiated, but rather is something that potentially divides subjects on the basis of their interests (e.g. rich/poor; male/female; urban/rural, etc.). Hence, consent as realised through the provision of public goods incorporates (and to some extent is predicated on) an element of physical or symbolic coercion (i.e. the ability to propagate a particular understanding of the common good).

Finally, political subjects may be rational agents in terms of the choices they make, but such choices are never infinite, hence rationality is always relative to the choices that are available to any particular agent. People do not necessarily consent to contribute corveé labour to a state-sponsored canal project because they know it is the best of all possible options for the management of water in their region. Rather, choices are made relative to the immediate costs and benefits of compliance. So, when speaking of consent, we need to consider the conditions of possibility that any particular political subject encounters. We need to ask how the choices available to different subjects related to their different subject positions. Minimally, in Blanton and Fargher's analysis, 'state principals' and 'tax-payers' faced different choices in premodern states and hence would have operated with different definitions of rational action. The key question is how different kinds of subjectivity were made rational within any given political configuration (*cf.* Smith 2004).

What, then, of our original question? Baines and Yoffee have raised a number of key points regarding the constitution of political authority. Importantly, such authority is embedded in, and legitimised by, a larger social (and frequently cosmological) order. Yet, Baines and Yoffee's exclusive focus on 'high culture' as the producer of this order leaves us with a difficult dichotomy. It seems that we have only elite consent on one hand and the bare coercion of non-elites (or worse – nothing at all) on the other. In contrast, Blanton and Fargher have argued that, as rational agents, the consent of subjects is essential to the constitution of political authority in any context. Yet, as we have seen, assuming that this consent is a simple matter of balancing the interests of individual rational actors leaves unanswered most of the questions raised in Chapter One regarding the virtual nature of political authority and the intimate relationship it engenders between coercion and consent. Thinking systematically about this intimate relationship is no easy task. In particular, one needs relatively precise analytical tools and concepts in order to understand how political authority can rest on both coercion and consent, how it can serve both to dominate and to incorporate subaltern populations (who themselves may both accept and resist political authority) and how it can simultaneously reflect, select and shape cultural practices. Developing such analytical tools was a central concern of Antonio Gramsci's richly enigmatic political writings. Hence, a brief foray into Gramsci's thought will prove an essential digression in our exploration of transcendent political authority.

Antonio Gramsci

Antonio Gramsci was an Italian intellectual and political activist who played a leading role in the Italian Communist Party and was jailed by Mussolini from 1926 until just before his death in 1937. Gramsci is best known for the notebooks he kept while in prison, in which he attempted to think through in very broad terms what would be required to establish a proletarian state in Italy. In doing so, Gramsci felt it was necessary to understand the general failure of working-class revolutionary movements in the industrialised West, and the general resilience of the 'bourgeois' state in the face of numerous political and economic crises in the decade following the First World War. This process caused him to give particular attention to the relationship between the state, culture, leadership and power. Gramsci's approach to these issues charted a distinct path marked by his commitment to the class analysis of orthodox Marxism on one hand and to historicism, with its emphasis on concrete historical circumstances and human volition, on the other (Morera 1990).

While this is not the place, nor am I the scholar, to present an extended discussion of Gramsci's thought, one can gain a basic appreciation of his contribution to political theory through considering a number of key terms to which Gramsci's main ideas are linked. In particular, these are 'Hegemony', 'Intellectuals', 'Common Sense' and 'Historical Bloc'.

Hegemony, coercion and the state

For Gramsci, the key to understanding the state, both as something to overcome and as something to perfect, was to consider not only the administrative apparatus of a polity but also the social totality that supported and reproduced that polity. As he writes:

> … the State is the entire complex of practical and theoretical activities with which the ruling class not only justifies and maintains its dominance, but manages to win the active consent of those over whom it rules. (Gramsci 1971: 244)

For Gramsci, political society is the formal apparatus of government, and especially the seat of coercive powers, while civil society is the apparently private world outside of this formal apparatus, which none the less is intimately linked to it. Gramsci expresses this relationship in the simple formula: 'state = political society + civil society, in other words hegemony protected by the armour of coercion' (Gramsci 1971: 263).

The organic relation between political and civil society is most evident in constituting the consent of subjects to being ruled. For example, Gramsci writes:

> The State does have and request consent, but it also 'educates' this consent, by means of the political and syndical associations: these, however, are private organisms, left to the private initiative of the ruling class. (Gramsci 1971: 259)

As a number of scholars have shown (Laclau and Mouffe 2001: 7–41), Gramsci borrowed the term hegemony from Russian Social

Democracy, where it referred to the ideological leadership of the proletariat over other aligned groups (e.g. the peasantry). Yet in Gramsci's hands the concept was greatly expanded as a tool for analysis. To understand Gramsci's particular use of the term hegemony it is important to remember that his interests were both analytical and utopian. He wanted to understand the Italian state as an historical formation, and he wanted to facilitate the overthrow of that state and eliminate its necessity through the transformation of Italian society. As a result, Gramsci used hegemony to refer quite directly to the process by which subaltern classes acquiesced to their own political domination by ruling classes through the use of education, cultural activity, symbolic expression, religion, language, traditional cross-class alliances, etc. Under these circumstances, hegemony and coercion were intimately linked as two sides of the coin by which class dominance was organised and perpetuated. At the same time, he also used hegemony to refer to the process by which the subaltern classes could realise their own potential through a 'political-ethical' state that organised and articulated the classless civil society that would arise from the restructuring of the relations of production. Such a 'political-ethical' state would eliminate the need for the coercive powers of political society as it would (in what could only be described as a transcript of one of Foucault's nightmares):

> ... construct within the husk of political society a complex and well-articulated civil society, in which the individual can govern himself without his self-government thereby entering into conflict with political society – but rather becoming its normal continuation, its organic complement. (Gramsci 1971: 268)

Regardless of what one thinks of Gramsci's utopian vision, it is clear that his view of hegemony was quite different from how it is frequently characterised in academic circles, and reflected second-hand in anthropological and archaeological literature (see Kurtz 1996; Crehan 2002). For example, Gramsci's hegemony is not a kind of false consciousness embedded in the taken-for-granted order of tradition

(e.g. symbols, values, modes of communication); that to say an unrec-
ognised generative force lying behind cultural practices (e.g. Alonso
1994; Comaroff and Comaroff 1991: 22–32). Similarly, Gramsci's use
of consent did not simply confuse the so-called 'public' and 'hidden'
transcripts of the oppressed (*contra* Scott 1990: 95). Rather, for
Gramsci, hegemony entailed the organisation, direction, education
and articulation of the historical reality of a given class experience.
Hence, for the bourgeoisie, the form their hegemony took via the
modern state (apparently in either its liberal or its fascist form) was
an organic expression of their historical reality, just as the proletarian
'political-ethical' state would be for a future classless society. This
clearly complicates the concept of hegemony, making it much more
than the manufacture of consent. However, it also creates problems
for the analytical side of Gramsci's task, namely understanding how
and why subaltern classes would acquiesce to a hegemony that was
not an expression of their own historical reality. Clearly, coercion is
one of the answers, but it is an insufficient answer even in Gramsci's
own terms. This problem is never directly acknowledged or addressed
in Gramsci's writings; however, as is often the case, he provides the
tools for constructing an alternative 'neo-Gramscian' view in his
own passing comments and historical and cultural analysis. This will
become more evident if we turn to his use of the terms 'intellectuals'
and 'common sense'.

Intellectuals and common sense

Gramsci uses the term intellectual in an unusual way, one that links it
very strongly with the constitution of hegemony. For Gramsci, intellectuals were not defined by the nature of their activities, so much as
by their position in a system of social relations.

> All men are intellectuals ... but not all men have in society the function
> of intellectuals ... Thus there are historically formed specialised
> categories for the exercise of the intellectual function. (Gramsci 1971:
> 9–10)

This 'intellectual function' is the leading, educating and articulating of group hegemony. According to Gramsci, intellectuals are not simply generated by and for the state, but arise organically within fundamental social groups, a term he used in place of class when avoiding censorship in prison (Gramsci 1971: 5n. 1). Intellectuals in this sense can be engaged in a wide range of activities (e.g. technical or administrative) not typically viewed as intellectual in and of themselves, but which none the less provide a class with '… homogeneity and an awareness of its own function not only in the economic but also in the social and political fields' (Gramsci 1971: 50). However, Gramsci also notes that for dominant groups intellectuals act as 'deputies' in exercising '… the functions of social hegemony and political government' (Gramsci 1971: 12). These functions correspond in the first instance to '[t]he "spontaneous" consent given by the great masses of the population to the general direction imposed on social life by the dominant funda-mental group' and in the second to '[t]he apparatus of state coercive power which "legally" enforces discipline on those groups who do not "consent" either actively or passively' (Gramsci 1971: 12).

The effects of coercion and the appeal of a coherent vision of one's own life circumstances require little explanation, the '"spontaneous" consent of the great masses' is, however, more difficult to under-stand. Gramsci's immediate answer is that consent is caused by the '… prestige (and consequent confidence) which the dominant group enjoys because of its position and function in the world of production' (Gramsci 1971: 12). This explanation seems inadequate, except perhaps as a form of economic coercion. However, Gramsci himself reveals an alternative answer when he turns his attention to the specific task of shaping a hegemony of, and for, Italy's subaltern classes using the 'raw materials' of popular culture (termed 'common sense').

Gramsci was an orthodox Marxist in his belief that relations of production were the most fundamental to the shaping of history and society, and that capitalist relations of production in particular contained inherent contradictions that would lead to their demise. However, Gramsci also resisted determinism and hence argued against the 'fatalistic' view that such historical changes would happen on their own, or that historical associations and established understandings of the world would change quickly and automatically with changes in the relations of production. Hence, in Gramsci's view, intellectuals (in the form of the Communist Party) had to take an active role in shaping a new hegemony of, and for, the subaltern classes. In Gramsci's mind this involved the transformation of what he calls 'common sense', by which he means the unsystematised practical consciousness of the masses. For Gramsci, the everyday culture of the subaltern classes was limited in being unconscious, uncritical and unsystematic. It was not that people were unaware of their circumstances, but rather that this awareness was limited by its narrow focus and its combination with a 'hodge-podge' of contradictory ideas and orientations historically inherited and/or adopted from dominate groups (e.g. Gramsci 1971: 326–7). Most particularly, in the case of Italy, this included Catholicism. The task of intellectuals was not to remake 'common sense' but rather to construct a critical hegemony authentic to the political and economic realities of subaltern classes, using the raw materials of 'common sense' (those parts that Gramsci called 'good sense'). As Gramsci writes: '… it is not a question of introducing from scratch a scientific form of thought into everyone's individual life, but of renovating and making "critical" an already existing activity' (Gramsci 1971: 330–1). Certainly, in Gramsci's mind, hegemonic orders could not simply be concocted but had to connect with the shared experiences of those being led. As he states:

> It is evident that this kind of mass construction cannot just happen 'arbitrarily', around any ideology, simply because of the formally constructive will of a personality or a group … (Gramsci 1971: 341)

For Gramsci, then, hegemony is realised in continuous collective action and a common orientation. This occurs when intellectuals are able to draw out and make coherent problems and orientations of practical experiences found in an inchoate form in the realm of 'common sense'.

Importantly, for our purposes, Gramsci does not limit this method for constituting hegemony to the future Communist task of constituting what he certainly believed to be an authentic subaltern hegemony. For example, he states that '[e]very relationship of "hegemony" is necessarily an educational relationship', and that '[t]his form of relationship occurs between intellectual and non-intellectual sections of the population, between rulers and the ruled, between *élites* and their followers, leaders and led, the vanguard and the body of the army' (Gramsci 1971: 350). Gramsci also acknowledges that the 'man-in-the mass' can have a contradictory consciousness, one shaped by his practical activities in the realm of production, which would link him in common cause with other workers, and another that is 'superficially explicit, or verbal, which he has inherited from the past and uncritically absorbed' (Gramsci 1971: 333). Gramsci goes on to note that:

> ... this verbal conception is not without consequences. It holds together a specific social group, it influences moral conduct and the direction of will, with varying efficacy but often powerfully enough to produce a situation in which the contradictory state of consciousness does not permit any action, any decision or choice, and produces a condition of moral and political passivity. (Gramsci 1971: 333)

Hence, for Gramsci, all forms of hegemony involve a process of articulating and making coherent symbols, values, problems and material orientations inchoately present in 'common sense'. This is what gives hegemony its evocative power to elicit either active or passive consent. The difference between what Gramsci would consider a 'progressive' hegemony and a 'reactionary' one lies in which aspects of 'common sense' are brought forward and articulated as the basis of a social order. Hence, no form of hegemony ever articulates all possible values, problems and orientations – indeed, hegemonic projects actively select, ignore or even repress the multiple possibilities inherent in any lived historical context. It follows, then, that 'common sense' always contains within itself the possibility of constituting alternative or counter-hegemonies (see Laclau and Mouffe 2001: 105–14 for a similar understanding of Gramsci).

All of this might be well and good as a commentary on Gramsci's writings, but does it really help us understand political authority in the past and how this might be investigated through archaeological means? In particular, is Gramsci's conception of hegemony not just another example of deterministic Marxist thinking, reducing dynamic historical realities into the repetitive shadow play of class conflict? What does one do in non-capitalist contexts where relations of production may be comparatively simple, or where kinship, ethnicity and status seem to be at least as important as class in the organisation of political power?

There is no doubt that Gramsci saw relations of production as the most fundamental social relations, and he never broke with the belief that such relations would ultimately form the basis for hegemonic formations. However, as Ernesto Laclau and Chantal Mouffe (2001) have shown at some length, Gramsci's historicism and his active approach to the constitution of hegemony meant that the class character of agents in his analysis was never guaranteed in advance, but had to be constituted. We have already quoted Gramsci to the effect that people can possess a contradictory consciousness (e.g. verbal vs material), with distinct implications for how they view their own historical position and how they engage in political activity. In Gramsci's words, '[c]ritical understanding of self takes place therefore through a struggle of political "hegemonies", and of opposing directions …' (Gramsci 1971: 333). Gramsci, however, goes even further than this in his conception of the 'historical bloc'.

Historical bloc

For Gramsci, an 'historical bloc' represents 'the unity of the process of reality' (Gramsci 2000: 193). Here Gramsci is emphasising the unity in any given historical moment of factors generally distinguished as structures (forces and relations of production) or superstructures (most everything else).

As Gramsci states:

> The analysis of these propositions tends, I think, to reinforce the conception of 'historical bloc' in which precisely material forces are the content and ideologies are the form, though this distinction between form and content has purely indicative value, since the material forces would be inconceivable historically without form and the ideologies would be individual fancies without the material forces. (Gramsci 1971: 377)

In places, Gramsci portrays this unity in relatively mechanistic ways, with superstructural elements conforming to, rather than affecting, structural ones, as in his comparison of an historical bloc to human anatomy, where superstructure is the skin and structural relations the skeleton (Gramsci 2000: 197). Elsewhere, he describes an historical bloc more realistically as an ensemble of historical relationships in which '... the complex, contradictory and discordant ensemble of the superstructures is the reflection of the ensemble of the social relations of production' (Gramsci 1971: 366). As a political activist, Gramsci believed that identifying and transforming the structural relations reflected in the 'complex, contradictory and discordant ensemble of the superstructures', required ideological activity (see Gramsci 1971: 365–7, 375–7). In other words, superstructure (e.g. ideology) could in fact shape and change structure (e.g. relations of production), not least because in an 'historical bloc' these were dialectically, rather than merely causally, linked.

The historical bloc gains further significance when Gramsci links it to his interesting, if underdeveloped, relational theory of human subjectivity. For Gramsci, the subject exists as a node in a network of complex relationships. As he states:

> Man is to be conceived as an historical bloc of purely individual and subjective elements and of mass [i.e. collective] and objective or material elements with which the individual is in an active relationship. ... the synthesis of the elements constituting individuality is 'individual', but it cannot be realised and developed without

an activity directed outward, modifying external relations both with
nature and, in varying degrees, with other men, in the various social
circles in which one lives ... (Gramsci 1971: 360)

The implications of this perspective are multiple. First, the question
of whether or not hegemony has a necessary class character is largely
misplaced with regards to Gramsci's political thought. In so far as
particular relations of production exist as part of the nexus of social
and material relations that constitute individual subjectivity, then class
is latent in that historical bloc. There is no guarantee, however, that it is
this class experience that will be selected, brought forward and articulated in constituting any particular hegemonic order.

The second implication of Gramsci's historical bloc is that, in so far
as hegemony is part of the network of relations constituting individual
subjects, it can have a recursive relationship with 'common sense'. In
other words, everyday life is not simply a primordial generator of social
and cultural resources to be selected and articulated in constituting
hegemony, it is also shaped historically by the existence of hegemonic
orders. Hence, hegemonic orders can be reinscribed on everyday life as
an historical experience.

Applying Gramsci

A Gramscian perspective involves analysing the formation of hegemony
as a social (and indeed cosmological) order through the selective
articulation of cultural resources embedded in everyday life, such that
specific interests are disseminated as general (and indeed essential)
interests. Because hegemony articulates values, symbols, practices and
institutions that are intimately linked to people's lives, it often 'rings
true' in terms of emotions, experiences or necessities of everyday
life and hence forms a basis for voluntary consent to political and
economic domination. At the same time, because the formation of
hegemony is, by definition, partial (i.e. selective), it is never secure and
is always open to resistance or reformulation. Hence, the continued
reproduction of hegemony is intimately linked to relations of physical

and symbolic coercion. One could say, therefore, that hegemony defines the possibilities of consent, while force defines its limits. Finally, because both everyday culture (Gramsci's 'common sense') and hegemony are historically constituted, the experience of hegemonic power can be reinscribed into everyday life as a cultural resource. It follows, however, that the specific uses made of such reinscribed hegemony are potentially open.

A Gramscian approach to political authority clearly incorporates Baines and Yoffee's concern for order, legitimacy and wealth in early civilisations, while at the same time providing a means of understanding how such orders could relate to both elite and non-elite experiences of everyday life. A Gramscian approach would seem, therefore, well suited to addressing the question of how political authority was made transcendent in given contexts, in terms of both theory and practical application. This said, several points remain to be clarified if we are to effectively link our discussion of Gramsci to the issues and case studies discussed elsewhere in this book.

It should be clear that what we called political authority in Chapter One relates to what Gramsci termed political society. It is the seat, therefore, of coercive powers in Gramsci's equation. While Gramsci gave much attention to the constitution of hegemony in civil society, he gave little attention to the constitution of political society or its coercive powers, taking their existence for granted. Yet, as David Kertzer notes with regards to coercion,

> [T]hese sorts of power to constrain are not simply, or even essentially, a physical power, for they presuppose a symbolic power. The power of the government to compel people to act in certain ways is based on its ability to mobilize people to do its bidding. (Kertzer 1996: 3)

In essence, therefore, the coercive powers of political society must themselves be constituted as an aspect of hegemony. Here we can begin to see how the practices and strategies of political authority, coercive force and transcendent identification intersect and reinforce one another under the umbrella of hegemony as a moral order.

A second clarification relates to Gramsci's conception of intellectuals. Gramsci was of course correct to identify the existence of historically and culturally defined roles where the intellectual functions (selecting, ordering, articulating, interpreting) of hegemony are concentrated (e.g. priest, general, scribe, scientist, politician), and one might productively revisit archaeological discussions of elites, administrators or specialists by means of Gramsci's discussion of intellectuals. However, limiting the intellectual function of hegemony to these roles misses much of the important hegemonic work done on a day-to-day basis by virtually everyone. Indeed, for archaeologists it seems more productive to focus on intellectual products (texts, buildings, art, material symbols, administrative systems, etc.) that select, order and articulate cultural resources, rather than on intellectuals. This is more than just a case of making the most of archaeology's inconvenient absences. Rather, such a focus shifts our attention directly to material practices. For example, in the case of Shang oracle bones, there is no question that intellectuals in Gramsci's sense are at the centre of this practice. However, so too are the bones themselves, their preparation, processing and interpretation. Treating these simply as materialisations of already existing power (e.g. Demarrais et al. 1996) ignores the historical specificity of the practices involved and thereby misunderstands the materiality by which hegemony is constituted.

For the archaeologist, one last problem derives from Gramsci himself, as it is clear that he viewed his theory of hegemony as relevant only to modern societies. As he writes:

> In the ancient and mediaeval State alike, centralisation, whether political-territorial or social ... was minimal. The state was, in a certain sense, a mechanical bloc of social groups ... within the circle of political-military compression, which was only exercised harshly at certain moments, the subaltern groups had a life of their own, their own institutions etc. The modern state substitutes for the mechanical bloc of social groups their subordination to the active hegemony of the directive and dominant group. (Gramsci 1971: 54n. 4)

Ironically, Gramsci's view would seem rather close to that of Baines and Yoffee, in that hegemonic activity in ancient states is presumed to be limited by social fragmentation (*cf.* Giddens 1985; see Routledge 2003 for a critique), while social cohesion rests largely on the irregular exercise of bare force. As we have already seen, such a view of premodern political authority fails to account for its embeddedness in widely shared cultural practices and values. Such practices are clearly selected, developed and at times transformed almost beyond recognition; however, they still signal a degree of reciprocal interaction that remains unaccounted for in exclusively elite-centred views. Instead of presuming that the absence of a mass public culture means the absence of hegemonic activity, it is more interesting and relevant to ask how hegemonic orders are achieved in spite of, or even by means of, 'a mechanical bloc of social groups' (see Routledge 2003). Indeed, this is precisely what we intend to do in the next chapter as we look closely at the Imerina Kingdom of nineteenth-century Madagascar in order to understand how hegemony made possible the transcendence of political authority and, at the same time, served as a site for resisting and contesting that authority.

3

Hegemony in action

The kingdom of Imerina in central Madagascar

I see the numerous firenena across the land, they are all mine, I love them all, but I will mix hairs as I please.

Andrianampoinimerina, King of Imerina (Larson 2000: 178)

In an extremely interesting article, Susan Kus and Victor Raharijaona (2000) detail the intimate relationship between standard house plans amongst the Merina of highland Madagascar and the representation of kingship under Merina rulers of the nineteenth century. In particular, the singular authority of the ruler came to be embodied in the central pillar (*andry*) of the national palace, just as *andry* in Merina houses could serve as a symbol and an index of the household head. This subtle appropriation and transformation of common-sense understandings of the world fits rather well with the Gramscian perspective outlined in the previous chapter. Indeed, almost every aspect of Merina royal policy, from state ritual, through royal building programmes to royal labour service, can be understood as having selected and transformed widely shared Merina traditions in the interest of constituting and reproducing the hegemony of Merina sovereigns. For this reason, the kingdom of Imerina provides an excellent case study through which to explore the question of hegemony, raised in an abstract form in the previous chapter.

History and archaeology of Imerina

The kingdom of Imerina was located in central highland Madagascar and is best known for its rapid expansion by conquest between AD 1780 and 1830 (Figure 3.1). At its peak, Imerina incorporated about two-thirds of the island of Madagascar (c. 380,000 km^2) and a population of upwards of one million people (Campbell 2005: 136–7; Raison-Jourde 1991: 34). Information on this period of expansion comes from a variety of sources. The most important indigenous source is probably the transcriptions of royal oral histories made in the 1860s and known as the *Tantara* (*Tantara ny Andriana* = 'the Histories of Kings'; Callett 1908). European sources include travel accounts of merchants, slavers, and missionaries as well as military and ambassadorial personnel. Archaeological surveys and limited excavations have been carried out in parts of central Madagascar with some regularity since the 1970s, although both geographic and chronological coverage remains uneven. In what follows, I have relied on secondary sources that make use of the above primary sources, with the exception of some of the archaeological evidence.

Imerina is the name of the territory of one of Madagascar's major cultural groups, the Merina. The early history of both Madagascar's settlement and the settlement of its interior highland is uncertain and subject to controversy (see Kent 1970). For our purposes, the period prior to the eighteenth century is not immediately relevant except for one key aspect of Merina oral histories. According to the Merina, their ancestors displaced a group called the *Vazimba* in order to claim Imerina. As a result, *Vazimba* ancestors were viewed as playing an important role in the landscape of Imerina as sources of undomesticated and antagonistic primordial power associated with water, rocks and the underworld (see Bloch 1986: 42–3; 1987: 280; Kus and Raharijaona 1998: 61–4) .

The economy of highland Madagascar is based on riziculture in valleys and on terraced slopes. A key ecological factor is that large sections of these valleys were swampy and required labour-intensive

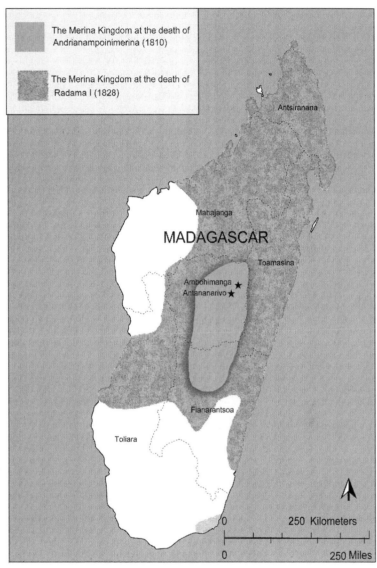

Figure 3.1 Map of the Kingdom of Imerina

drainage projects via ditches and levees in order to be brought under rice cultivation (see Berg 1981; Campbell 2005: 18–30). In Merina tradition, kingship is closely associated with the initiation of such drainage projects, most notably the king Andriamasinavalona ('The Noble finely enveloped by sanctity'), who may have reigned at the turn of the eighteenth century and was credited with both the unification of Imerina and an extensive restoration and expansion of the rice cultivation zone. Archaeological evidence in the form of survey data from north-eastern Imerina (western Avaradrano) is more ambivalent on the scale and timing of these irrigation projects, with intensive rice cultivation evident from the end of the fifteenth century (Wetterstrom and Wright 2007: 286), but large-scale centralised irrigation not unambiguously attested until the end of the eighteenth century (Schwarz 2007: 295).

According to the *Tantara*, Andriamasinavalona could not decide between his children in choosing a successor and divided his kingdom into four parts on his death – these making up the four traditional provinces of the heartland of Imerina. This led to internecine warfare for three generations. European accounts provide support for the idea that the eighteenth century was a period of conflict and fragmentation (see Berg 1985; Larson 2000: 49–147). The rise of plantations in Mauritius and other Mascarene islands increased the intensity of slaving activities in highland Madagascar. With slaving came a more extensive introduction of muskets into warfare and the circulation of silver coinage. Rulers eager for silver and muskets actively sold both war captives and their own subjects into slavery. An increase in the tendency to demand tribute in silver rather than in kind, and the need to use silver to buy relatives out of slavery, seems to have put pressure on local descent groups, who became more mobile, smaller and more fluid in terms of membership and royal affiliation (Larson 2000: 156–7).

Archaeological research, at least in north-eastern Imerina, suggests that we need to be cautious in estimating the scale and universality of these social disruptions. Here the early eighteenth century sees a slowing of the previous century's very high rates of population growth, but no population decline (Dewar 2007: 101–3). Settlement patterns show considerable continuity, with an increase in the number of very small sites being the primary change. An increased prominence of fortifications at larger sites is the principal archaeological evidence complementing the historical evidence for civil war (Wright 2007: 108). At the same time, the limited scope and chronological precision of the available archaeological evidence also means that evidence for social disruption in the mid-eighteenth century may be obscured by latter developments, or better attested in regions that have not been subject to intensive archaeological investigation.

Starting in about 1780, Andrianampoinimerina ('The Noble desired in the heart of Imerina') used trade connections to build up silver and muskets in order to attract displaced followers and usurp his uncle as ruler of one of the four provinces. He then began a series of aggressive military campaigns that united Imerina, and began to expand its territory outward at the expense of its neighbours. Andrianampoinimerina attracted displaced descent groups, promising protection from slavers, while at the same time acquiring resources via the sale of war captives into slavery (see Berg 1985; Larson 2000: 147–56; Raison-Jourde 1991: 40–4).

Aggressive expansion peaked under Andrianampoinimerina's son Radama I, whose reign from ca. 1810 to 1828, saw tens of thousands die in wars of conquest, many of whom were conscripted Merina soldiers who died of fever and disease some distance from home (Larson 2000: 217–40). While taxation, especially in the form of uncut silver coins called *hasina* (which also means 'blessing'), was fiscally and symbolically important, Merina royalty relied at least as heavily on labour service. Under Radama I the extraction of labour service reached extreme levels, both via conscription into largely unpaid military service and via the extension of local obligations to a wider cross-section of the population to compensate for the young men absent in military service.

Unlike earlier periods, archaeological evidence from the late eighteenth and early nineteenth centuries shows dramatic changes very much in keeping with expectations derived from the documentary evidence. Long-established sites are abandoned and new settlements founded; primary and secondary centres grow considerably in size and are heavily fortified. For the first time, the old capital of Ambohimanga may have had a population larger than could be fed from its available catchment area, suggesting either a dependence on tax/tribute or the extension of rice cultivation through large-scale irrigation schemes (Schwarz 2007: 295). A line of fortified frontier settlements is now discernible in the far south of Imerina's traditional territory, and for the first time gun flints occur as regular finds in excavations (see Wright 2007: 89–90, 108–11).

Archaeological evidence also supports the documented tradition that, even while founding a new capital at Antananarivo, Andrianampoinimerina reconstructed the old capital of Ambohimanga as a ritual centre on a grand scale. He appears to have followed cosmologically significant spatial orientations in laying out the gates and fortifications (Kus 2007; Kus and Raharijaona 1998; Belrose-Huyghues 1983) and deployed monumental stonework in their construction, most particularly in the case of the stone discs used to block gates (Gabler 2007).

Finally, preliminary archaeological evidence from the region of Andrantsay, south-west of Imerina, seems to show evidence for Andrianampoinimerina's conquests (see Crossland 2001). Here the settlement pattern exhibits dramatic changes near the turn of the century, with most of the oldest, best fortified sites, at the highest elevations and with the most built tombs (both signs of higher status residents), being abandoned. About half of the settlements with ditch fortifications occupied in the nineteenth century appear to have been new foundations at the time of the Merina conquest (Crossland 2001: 834).

Radama I and his successors (with the exception of Queen Ranalova I) formed close ties with Great Britain via the London Mission Society. Under Ranalova I, state ritual was considerably elaborated, perhaps as a means of counter-balancing the spread of Christianity and European influence (Bloch 1986: 18–22). Her son and successor Radama II reversed these policies and in 1869 Protestant Christianity was adopted as the state religion during the reign of Ranalova II. British and French conflict over economically important colonial interests in the Mascerenes led to a French invasion of Madagascar and a bloody war from 1883 to 1885. During this invasion Britain remained uninvolved, essentially ceding Madagascar to the French sphere of influence in exchange for a free hand in other areas, such as Zanzibar (Ellis 1985: 32–3). Eventually, after widespread uprisings against the French from 1895 to 1899, the kingdom of Imerina was dissolved and replaced by a French colonial government (see Ellis 1985).

Ritual and the ideology of kingship

While a Merina polity, in some form or another, existed long before 1780, the *Tantara* gives particular attention to Andrianampoinimerina as the founder of a renewed Merina order. Stress is always placed upon the singularity of the ruler and the unity of Imerina, something that is symbolically represented over and over again in the deeds and words of Andrianampoinimerina (see Kus and Raharijaona 1998: 67–8; 2000: 104–6; Raison-Jourde 1991: 48–52). This key theme is summed up in the Malagasy proverb: 'When there are three lords there is famine and hunger, when there are two lords wives and children are lost as slaves, but when there is one sovereign children are chubby' (Veyrières and Mèritens 1967: 36, as quoted in Kus and Raharijaona 1998: 68). While there is certainly a rhetorical element to Andrianampoinimerina's prominence in the *Tantara*, the archaeological record clearly attests to the transformative nature of his reign.

As Maurice Bloch has argued on numerous occasions, this renewed Merina order revolved around royalty and was embodied and realised via public ritual. Two of the most prominent public rituals studied by Bloch are the ritual of the royal bath (Bloch 1987) and the circumcision ritual (Bloch 1986). In both cases, Bloch stresses the ways in which royal rituals incorporate and transform rituals, beliefs and values associated with local descent groups. Merina and other highland Madagascar groups tended to be organised into preferentially endogamous, bilateral descent groups that ideally share rights in land and residence in villages. These were known in the nineteenth century as *firenena* and were ranked in social status based on genealogical distance from key royal figures in the distant past. Major status divisions were between so-called 'nobles' or *andriana* (from whom royalty could, at least notionally, arise), commoners or *hova*, and slaves. One long-term dynamic of the Merina kingdom was a tension between the desire to embed royal hegemony within the moral order of descent groups, while at the same time to break down their autonomy as alternative centres of loyalty and identity.

Both the ritual of the royal bath and the circumcision ritual seem to represent royal appropriations of common Merina rituals (Bloch 1986: 116–18; 1987; Kus and Raharijaona 2001: 117–20). At the heart of both, for example, is the transference of blessings downwards from elders to juniors via the use of water associated with the *Vazimba* ancestors. Merina royalty were inserted into this chain of blessing by organising and centralising these rituals such that the sovereign served as the initiator of a national chain of blessing. In the case of the royal bath, the washing of the king's hair on the New Year initiated the replication of this ceremony down a line defined by status and seniority. It was also the occasion of annual visits to family tombs, linking in this way ancestors, descent and royalty. According to the *Tantara*, while declaring that he did not change the ways of the ancestors, Andrianampoinimerina decreed that circumcision rituals were to occur only once every seven years, and to be initiated by the king and carried out by descent groups in order of their status and seniority, starting with royal children (Bloch 1986: 113–17).

In a functional sense, Merina royalty justified its rule through ritual by placing itself in the most senior position in this chain of blessing, in essence nationalising the ranking structure of descent groups. Rather conveniently this included the reciprocal delivery of uncut silver coins (*hasina*) upwards along the same chain, and indeed both the royal bath and circumcision rituals served as occasions for the delivery of taxes and tribute to the sovereign. However, the role of such rituals in the constitution of political authority goes much further.

The symbolic content of both of these state rituals is complex and provides many examples of the appropriation and transformation of 'common sense' practices, symbols and values. For our purposes, one of the most striking is the way in which Merina royalty drew upon the undomesticated power of the *Vazimba* ancestors. Regular Merina were dependent on their ancestors to neutralise, as it were, the wild powers inherent in water related to the *Vazimba*. Sovereigns, however, did not have ancestors in the same way as regular Merina, in the sense that they were singular, standing apart from descent groups and being buried in individual tombs (Kus and Raharijaona 2001). At the same time, Merina rulers could lay claim through the mythical founder of Imerina, Ralambo, to being both the conquerors of the *Vazimba* and their partial descendants, as Ralambo's mother was said to be a *Vazimba* queen. Hence, Merina royalty could partake of, and control, an undomesticated source of power that stood outside of Merina society as defined by ancestors and descent groups. In other words, the political authority of Merina rulers was not constituted from crude appropriations of popular symbols and rituals. Rather, it involved the transformation of those symbols and rituals by representing them in terms of a transcendent order, one that reinforced the wider hegemony of senior over junior kinsmen, while at the same time transcending this hegemony in the singular position of the ruler.

Bloch's analysis of Merina royal rituals gives us something of a structural model for the constitution of political authority in Gramscian terms; something that we might represent along the lines of: Appropriation → Transformation → Reinscription. This is conceptually useful, but it also rather static and fails to capture the historical dynamic of political authority as something that is both asserted and contested in relation to given hegemonic formations. Two examples from nineteenth-century Imerina will give us some sense of the dynamic nature of this process. The first is a single event involving a haircut, while the second is a longer-term process with a more clearly archaeological component, involving the development of burial practices.

Hegemony in action I: Radama I's haircut

Both Merina men and women wore their hair in elaborate plaits in the eighteenth and nineteenth centuries and had almost 30 terms for these hairstyles (Larson 2000: 240). One means by which war captives were distinguished on enslavement was by shearing their hair. Indeed, an eighteenth-century king of Marovatana, known for illegitimately enslaving his own subjects, was referred to as 'Mr. big scissors' (Larson 2000: 243).

The singularity of the king is also compared to his hairstyle, for, just as the various strands of the king's hairs were woven together and ultimately all attached to his head, so too were the various strands of the Merina woven together into a single, beautiful whole by the king (Larson 2000: 5–6, 178–9). However, in 1822, Radama I decided to cut his hair short in the style of his British military advisors who had helped him establish and train Imerina's first standing army (Figure 3.2). Public reaction to his haircut was divided. On one hand, many soldiers in Imerina's newly professionalised army, as well as officials and some mission-school students, followed Radama's lead and had (or were required to have) their own hair cut short as a sign of their affiliation with the king and his modernising regime. On the other hand, protest broke out most particularly amongst women, who led those stating that Radama I had become a slave of the British.

Hair as a symbol of descent group fertility was especially associated with women, as was the privilege of plaiting men's hair. A group of 4,000 women gathered to petition Radama to regrow his hair and sever his links with the British government. Interestingly, in their exchange, both Radama I and the protesting women grounded their arguments

RADAMA.

KING OF MADAGASCAR

London. Published by R. Bentley, 8, New Burlington Street, 1833.

Figure 3.2 Radama I (source: Owen 1833: 118)

in the hegemonic language of ancestral tradition. For the women, however, this implied constraints on the centralising and aggrandising behaviour of Radama, while for Radama his political innovations were justified by the traditional prerogative of Merina royalty to do as they pleased (Larson 2000: 248–9, 253). Rather strikingly, Radama is quoted as saying that whoever had brought this petition to him should be executed, as 'they have forbidden me to carry out my desire. What they have done prevents me from being king' (as quoted in Larson 2000: 250). In fact, Radama I is said to have gathered 2,000 soldiers, requiring them to swear that on the king's order they would put to death the instigators of these protests even if it were their own parents. He then singled out four leaders from amongst the protestors and ordered soldiers who were members of the women's own descent groups to bayonet them (Larson 2000: 252).

The king's hair may have been a royal symbol, straightforwardly ideological as a static representation of order. At the same time, it was also a language through which the limits of political authority were contested, and on which the coercive powers of the kingdom of Imerina were brought to bear (Larson 2000: 253–7). Here we can see hegemony in historically dynamic, rather than structural terms. As Larson (2000: 256) notes, in adopting the logic of royal hegemony in their protest Merina women were at a distinct disadvantage, yet at the same time this was the most potent moral force available to them in confronting the king.

Larson's point can be emphasised by considering Peter Gose's analysis of royal oracles in the Inca Empire (Gose 1996). Gose notes that the Inca tradition of mummifying and venerating dead kings in regional shrines, where these past rulers could then provide oracles of relevance to contemporary events, was a means of asserting and negotiating subaltern interests within the framework of absolute royal power. Because these oracles originated from his royal predecessors, rather than living subjects, they could be heeded without undermining the absolute rule of the reigning Inca. In the words of Peter Gose, '[o]racles made the king listen without having to listen to a rival.

Conversely, oracles gave those without power a voice, but not a voice of their own' (Gose 1996: 16). While the protests of Merina women occurred in a moment of political crisis, they share with Inca oracles the attempt to transform royal hegemony into a 'weapon of the weak' in James Scott's (1985) terms, even as its deployment served to reproduce that hegemony as a 'public transcript'.

Hegemony in action II: Tombs, kin and kings

What makes the story of Radama I's haircut all the more striking is that the moral order to which the protesting women appealed, one in which Merina kingship preserved and protected the world of descent groups and ancestors, is credited in its establishment to Radama I's father, Andrianampoinimerina. In the *Tantara* Andrianampoinimerina is credited with re-establishing the fixity of descent groups in Imerina, after the chaos of the eighteenth century. In particular, he is quoted to say that every descent group must return to its own land and ancestors and essentially stay put. Only the king, again using the metaphor of hair, was free 'to mix the hairs' of the Merina as he pleased by moving people from their ancestral land. Andrianampoinimerina is also credited with formalising the rank order of the various Merina descent groups, ascribing certain privileges on the basis of that order and empowering *fokonolona* (councils of elders) to adjudicate and make collective decisions within each descent group (Larson 2000: 180–2). Central to the fixing of descent groups in space was the construction of ancestral tombs (Figure 3.3). Andrianampoinimerina is credited with telling the Merina to build megalithic stone tombs to house their ancestors (Larson 2000: 184, 191). The construction of megalithic tombs, and especially the movement of their monumental stone slab walls, required considerable collective effort in the form of work teams, which in turn emphasised the shared solidarity of tomb-building groups (Kus and Raharijaona 1998: 58–9; Larson 2000: 188–90). As Susan Kus and Victor Raharijaona have pointed out (1998: 68, 73–4), this also created an experiential link between collective labour in the service of the ancestors, and labour service to Andrianampoinimerina. Such royal labour service focused on stone-moving projects, such as the erection of megalithic gate-stones in settlements fortified by the king, and in the large-scale renovation of the ancient capital, Ambohimanga. Interestingly, one factor that made the spatial orientation of Ambohimanga's gates cosmologically significant is that these same orientations were used in the construction of tombs and houses (Belrose-Huyghues 1983; Kus 2007; Kus and Raharijaona 1998: 72; 2000: 106).

Tombs also provided potent cultural resources to be contested in the reproduction of political authority. As noted above, visits to family tombs in order to rewrap the dead and receive blessings from the ancestors were incorporated into the annual state ritual of the royal bath (Bloch 1987). This practice was expanded outside of the Merina

ANCIENT TOMB.

Figure 3.3   Stone slab tomb, central Madagascar (source: Sibree 1870: 247)

heartland in conjunction with the expansion of the Merina state. At the same time, in contrast to family tombs, royal tombs were singular, not collective, and such tombs were built above ground rather than being semi-subterranean (Kus and Raharijaona 2001: 118). Monarchs were buried at night rather than at sunset, as they were the 'sun-that-is-not-two'. The ambiguity, indeed virtual denial, of royal mortality meant that the heir or heiress did not assume mourning clothes or participate in the funeral, but when he or she assumed office it was said that the 'sun was newly risen' (Kus and Raharijaona 2001: 118).

Archaeological surveys in north-eastern Imerina suggest that, although stone built tombs were not an invention of Andrianampoinimerina, there are marked changes in tomb construction that can be dated to the late eighteenth or early nineteenth century. Dating tombs in central Madagascar is problematic, in that tombs in continuously occupied sites were continuously modified. Looking only at newly founded sites with tombs, from each successive time period, Henry Wright and his colleagues were able to suggest that tombs constructed of very large horizontal and vertical slabs were a development of the late eighteenth–early nineteenth century, although these occur alongside already established construction methods, such as the use of dressed stone blocks (Wright 2007: 71–3). Interestingly, another development of the late eighteenth-early nineteenth centuries in north-eastern Imerina is a reduction in the proportion of sites containing tombs within the settlement boundaries and a greater correlation between the presence of interior tombs and other signs of settlement impor-tance (Wright 2007: 109). Documented Merina traditions, all of which post-date Andrianampoinimerina, suggest that only *adriana* (noble) descent groups had tombs within their settlements (Kus and Raharijaona 2001). Archaeological evidence might, therefore, support the *Tantara* tradition that the ordering and fixing of the relative status of descent groups was associated with the reign of Andrianampoinimerina and became embodied in traditions and privileges related to the nature and placement of family tombs.

The most famous aspect of Malagasy burial customs, the elaborate secondary burial ritual involving the handling and rewrapping of disarticulated ancestral bones at collective tombs termed *famadihana* (see Bloch 1971), was not initially the dominant mode of burial in Imerina. Although secondary burial is attested in eighteenth-century accounts, the *famadihana* in its present form only emerged towards the end of the nineteenth century, especially after the end of the Merina state (Raison-Jourde 1991: 711–21; Larson 2001). Its development is linked in part to a long struggle over burial between descent groups and rulers.

One of the ironies of the apparent strengthening of descent group identity and its attachment to specific ancestral places under the Merina state is that Merina rulers, and particularly Radama I, moved people away from their ancestral homelands on an unprecedented scale via military, labour and administrative service. In this context of military expansion, descent group identity became strongly focused on funerary rituals. In the early nineteenth century, secondary burial in family tombs was primarily the result of burying soldiers who had died in Imerina's wars of expansion (Larson 2001: 131–6). Funerary rites were preferentially for primary burial, with elaborate expenditure in terms of sacrificing bulls for feasts and equipping of the tomb with wealth in silver and household goods (Larson 2001: 139–42).

Françoise Raison-Jourde (1991: 714–15) credits the decline in primary burial rituals focused on wealth expenditure to the establishment of Christianity as the state religion under Ranalova II (reigned 1868–83), who banned the sacrifice of bulls at funerals as a pagan custom. However, royal resistance to elaborate funeral rituals can be traced back almost to the beginning of Imerina's expansion. Radama I is said to have opposed the effort expended by soldiers preparing and returning their comrades' bones, as well as the wealth being expended on funerals. He declared that soldiers should be buried where they died, encouraging them to view all of Imerina as their own country (Larson 2001: 134–5). Similarly, the expense of Radama's extensive military campaigning, combined with a marked decline in the availability of silver coinage following the banning of slave exports in 1820, led to something of a monetary crisis towards the end of Radama I's reign.

Hence, in 1824 he absolved the Merina of the obligation to repay loans taken out specifically for the purposes of holding funerary feasts and depositing the requisite amounts of wealth in tombs. This had the effect of making creditors unwilling to loan silver for the purposes of funerary rituals, keeping precious coinage in circulation and hence available for taxation (Larson 2001: 143–4). Radama I's campaign against the interment of wealth seems to stand in direct opposition to the *Tantara*'s tradition that Andrianampoinimerina encouraged the Merina to invest their wealth in collective tombs (Larson 2000: 191). Ironically, it also stands in direct opposition to Radama I's own funeral in 1828, which was said to include the burial of 10,300 silver coins and imported goods worth £60,000 with the king's body (Larson 2001: 144).

Over the course of the nineteenth century, political, economic and religious pressures encouraged descent groups to reduce their emphasis on displays of wealth in primary burial rituals, and to focus efforts on the elaboration of secondary burial rituals. Importantly, while the burial practices of kin groups developed in relation to royal (and later colonial) attempts to control them, the outcome of these changes was not necessarily what Merina rulers had envisioned. It seems that the hegemonic order in which the king made the land secure for the ancestors as exemplified in collective tombs also served to limit kingship and strengthen the independence of descent groups. Secondary burial in some form or another was a long-standing tradition in highland Madagascar, but the *famadihana* in its ethnographically famous form seems to have developed as part of long-term struggles between Merina royalty and Merina descent groups over the meaning and control of the central cultural resources of ancestors, tombs and wealth.

Summation

The history of Imerina provides a concrete example of how hegemony constitutes transcendent political authority by appropriating and transforming shared cultural resources embedded in what Gramsci called 'common sense'. Merina history also highlights the role of coercion, both in law and in physical force, as the limits of hegemony were reached through events like Radama I's haircut.

At the same time, the case of Imerina has also taken us beyond Gramsci in important ways. Gramsci's utopian goals meant that he gave little attention to the uses subaltern groups might make of actually existing hegemonic orders, as he viewed these as inauthentic to the experience of proletarians and peasants. Yet, as we saw in the case of Merina women and Inca oracles, existing hegemonic orders often provide the most powerful and pervasive arguments available to subaltern groups in the immediate context of conflict with authority. Hence, polity formation is not simply a case of domination on one side and revolution on the other. Rather, it involves on-going debate over what hegemonic orders do and do not include, framed by relations of force and carried out in contexts where cultural and material resources are not evenly distributed amongst participants. All of this involves material practices and contexts that are at least partially discernible in the archaeological record. It also involves much more than just politics. It is to this 'bigger picture' that we now turn.

4

Beyond politics

Articulation and reproduction in Athens and the Inca Empire

There are processes at work, therefore, that define regional spaces within which production and consumption, supply and demand (for commodities and labour power), production and realisation, class struggle and accumulation, culture and lifestyle, hang together as some kind of structured coherence within a totality of productive forces and social relations.

David Harvey (1985: 146)

On page 172 of the sixth edition of Renfrew and Bahn's (2012) widely used text book *Archaeology: theories, methods and practice* there is a table summarising the relationship between different social fields (i.e. social organisation, economic organisation, settlement pattern, religious organisation, architecture) and different levels of social organisation (i.e. mobile hunter-gatherer groups, segmentary society, chiefdom, state). Each cell in this table links a distinct social field with an overarching social form by means of a trait with archaeological implications. It is, in essence, a kind of pocket field guide to the identification of social evolution in the archaeological record. This, of course, is exactly the sort of thing against which the critics of neo-evolutionism have consistently railed; a view in which politics, economy and social relations are treated as attributes of some larger entity (a 'culture' or 'society') that has taken the phylogenetic form of the state. As noted in previous chapters, this unitary position assumes what it needs to explain; namely how sets of seemingly disparate words and actions, routines and spectacles, resources and beliefs constitute the virtual powers invoked by the phrase 'the state' (*cf.* Kurtz 2006). That said, Renfrew and Bahn's table has at least one clear advantage; it forcibly reminds us that political power encompasses much more than just politics.

Here is our problem. If we begin from a cross-cultural and transhistorical perspective, it is difficult to identify necessary and consistent relationships between political power and other aspects of life that do not trivialise the lived realities of specific historical contexts. Centralised powers do not always mobilise resources in the same way, not least because they hold no consistent relationship with the realm of production (not to mention distribution or consumption). Furthermore, one cannot point to a common mode, or degree, of integration when it comes to the relationship between domestic groups or communities, and hierarchical polities. Indeed, even the boundary between rulers and ruled is not acknowledged, defined or represented consistently across time and space.

The incoherence of human society as a general category underlies the failure of unitary views of the state as a social or institutional form. It is why social evolutionists are forever fated to choose between reductionism and taxonomy when faced with the diversity of human social life. However, acknowledging the incoherence of human society as a general category presents us with a definite problem, namely how then do we explain the apparent coherence of specific social formations?

To be more precise; when sovereignty is reproduced in any specific historical context, it requires the assembly of a whole range of key elements into relationships that are neither wholly determinate nor wholly independent. Modes of production, accumulation and consumption, modes of identification and differentiation (e.g. kinship, gender, age and status), domestic, task and interest group composition, not to mention technologies, objects, landscapes and taskscapes, are all examples of elements whose interrelationship can be central to the reproduction of sovereignty in given contexts. This does not mean that, for example, politics subsumes economic production or vice versa. What it does mean is that the practices, strategies and relationships of sovereignty must bring politics and economic production together and take account of each, however imperfectly. This strategic process of assembly, of articulating elements in a manner that makes sovereignty possible, is another way of understanding hegemony. Such acts of assembly are never guaranteed, but must be achieved actively and strategically in specific places under specific historical circumstances. This makes it rather interesting and important to explore how, in given contexts, the relevant elements 'hang together' to form a 'spatio-temporal fix' (Jessop 2006) giving particular realisations of sovereignty whatever stability and durability they may possess.

In this chapter I want to go beyond the more obvious issues of demarcating and asserting political power that have concerned us thus far in order to explore how it is that things 'hang together' in specific historical contexts and how this relates to hegemony and sovereignty. Common answers that depend on static, stable or holistic views of society, such as homeostasis or functional interdependence, have been extensively and effectively critiqued in the archaeological literature (e.g. Shanks and Tilley 1988: 138–41). So too have explanations rooted in methodological individualism, such as rational choice theory, that posit a priori universal human subjects with fixed hierarchies of desire (see Johnson 2006 with responses). Equally problematic are perspectives that seem to valorise unconstrained agency (see Johnson 2006 with responses), as if the indeterminacy of human social life meant that specific human lives were all equally indeterminate and unconstrained.

More interesting are approaches that actively struggle with the problem of determinacy and contingency in given social formations. One place to start is with Marxism's, and especially Western Marxism's, long struggle with the problem of economic determinism and historical contingency (Jay 1984). As we noted in Chapter 2, this tension was a central concern of Antonio Gramsci in developing his concept of an historical bloc as 'the unity of the process of reality' (Gramsci 2000: 193). Gramsci's insistence that material forces and ideologies were inseparably realised in given historical blocs partially dissolved the orthodox Marxist (i.e. the Second International) division between a society's determining economic base and its determined ideological superstructure. At the same time, Gramsci located the realisation of an historical bloc not at the abstract level of society, but rather in the formation of specific human subjects who exist at the intersection of material forces, history, social relations, ideologies and individuality. In doing so he introduced a sophisticated and penetrating means of addressing what might be termed the contingent determinacy of specific historical contexts (see Gramsci 1971: 352–60).

One drawback to Gramsci's formulation, already noted in Chapter 2, is that it retains an essential core of economic determinism. For Gramsci, an historical bloc is simultaneously the contingent outcome of specific historical conjunctures and pre-determined as the logical outcome of the relations and forces of production. It is rather difficult to 'have one's cake and eat it too' in this manner, hence it is useful to consider approaches that help us extend the concept of historical bloc beyond Gramsci.

In their 'post-Marxist' manifesto *Hegemony and socialist strategy*, Ernesto Laclau and Chantal Mouffe (2001) explicitly sought to root out Gramsci's residual essentialism by means of post-structuralist discourse theory. For example, in their terms a 'social and political space relatively unified through the instituting of nodal points and the constitution of *tendentially* relational identities is what Gramsci called a historical bloc' (Laclau and Mouffe 2001: 136, emphasis in original). Here the phrase '*tendentially* relational' is significant because Laclau and Mouffe recognise no necessary or fixed identities or social relation-ships. For them, the social world is overdetermined, in the sense of always containing multiple possibilities that prevent it from being fully intelligible in a fixed form. Hence, there is no society in the sense of a singular totality. Instead, there are only ongoing attempts to differen-tiate elements from within the social world's myriad of possibilities and articulate them together in a discursive formation around some privi-leged nodal point, thereby seeking to transform and fix their identity with regard to each other (Laclau and Mouffe 2001: 105–14). In Laclau and Mouffe's formulation an element can be virtually anything (a practice, person, category, object, etc.) that is discursively recognised as a 'difference' in the linguistic sense. Laclau and Mouffe consider such discursive formations to be hegemonic formations when they are shaped in terms of antagonistic forces, that is to say, in terms of the subordination or exclusion of oppositional positions.

Laclau and Mouffe do not really answer the question of why things 'hang together' within an historical bloc; rather, they redefine what it means to 'hang together'. Hence, at this abstract level social, formations are entirely contingent. In part this is because Laclau and Mouffe actively deny that causes can be external to given discursive formations, as would be the case in the orthodox Marxist precept that relations and forces of production shape human consciousness and social forms. In so far as they might answer our question, it would need to be in terms of the internal dynamics of given historical blocs; yet here one finds their analysis impoverished in at least two ways.

First, Laclau and Mouffe deny the existence of non-discursive practices, using Wittgenstein's concept of language games (Laclau and Mouffe 2001: 108) to deny that mental and material activities can be segregated in this manner. Objects exist, but they cannot interact with humans except through the discourse that makes them evident. Here, Laclau and Mouffe could learn much from Actor-Network Theory, an approach with which they otherwise share many parallels.

At about the same time that the first edition of Laclau and Mouffe's book was published, Actor-Network Theory (ANT) began to take shape within Science Studies through the work of scholars such as Bruno Latour, Michel Callon and John Law. ANT sought to develop radically empirical descriptions of science and technology as networks of relations between actors without presuming in advance what constituted an actor (e.g. human v. non-human; organic v. inorganic; organism v. institution) or privileging causes conceived as external to the network (e.g. power, social structure, economy – all of which would be seen as network effects, not causes, in ANT).

ANT makes little or no direct use of either Gramsci or Laclau and Mouffe. However, like Laclau and Mouffe, ANT scholars tend to deny society as an entity, and argue that the social exists only in the process of assembling relational networks of actors (Latour 2005); that such networks are contingent and heterogeneous (Law 1992; Latour 2005); and that the agency of actors is constituted within, rather than prior to, such networks (Law 1992).

Where a major difference lies is in the active agency that ANT ascribes to the material world. This is not simply a case of discursive fancy bumping up against cold hard facts. In ANT the natural world is as indeterminate and rife with hidden possibilities as is the social world (indeed they are the same world!). Furthermore, these emergent possibilities only reveal themselves in relation to other human and non-human actors, that is to say, within specific networks. However, these acts of revelation are not merely the result of human discursive recognition (e.g. the cluster of practices, discourses and identities that arose with the identification and naming of AIDS). Rather, the material world itself has a kind of agency in that the qualities and affordances of different configurations of matter (and other non-human actors) shape how humans relate to, and by means of, these different non-human entities (e.g. the specific qualities and affordances of HIV have made an obvious difference to the cluster of practices, discourses and identities linked to AIDS).

Power, therefore, is not merely reflected or 'materialised' in matter. Power is a quality of networks linking human and non-human actors as mediators or intermediators in a chain of interactions. Bruno Latour, for example, is fond of citing the intense, time-consuming, face-to-face interactions that are required to build and maintain relations of dominance in troops of baboons where, in comparison with human relations, the material mediators constituting power are very limited. As he states:

> If sociologists had the privilege to watch more carefully baboons repairing their constantly decaying 'social structure', they would have witnessed what incredible cost has been paid when the job is to

maintain, for instance, social dominance with no *thing* at all, just social skills … It's the power exerted through entities that don't sleep and associations that don't break down that allows power to last longer and expand further … (Latour 2005: 70, emphasis in original)

This symmetrical (to use an ANT term) appreciation of the mediatory role of the material world is missing from Laclau and Mouffe, and yet the agency of matter in relation to human beings is certainly a key factor in why things 'hang together' in specific contexts. This is because networks and discursive formations are not merely sets of relations, they are also sets of material interdependencies.

For the real import of this point to become clear, however, we must introduce a second factor missing from Laclau and Mouffe and also from most of the ANT literature, namely the historical component of Gramsci's historical bloc. To quote Stuart Hall's sympathetic critique of Laclau and Mouffe: 'Their problem isn't politics but history. They have let slip the question of the historical forces which have produced the present, and which continue to function as constraints and determinations on discursive articulation' (in Grossberg 1986: 58). Material forces and ideologies gain their ability to shape and constrain not through universal relationships of causation but through historical relationships of emerging material interdependence. Living in particular environments, utilizing particular technologies, being born into the midst of existing practices, dispositions and values, means that over time social fields are linked to one another, the possibilities of existence for specific subjects are constrained, and life choices gain an element of path dependency. By selecting and articulating existing elements in a given historical context, hegemonic projects attempt to capitalise on these material interdependences in the interest of forming and reproducing sovereignty.

In the remainder of this chapter I want to explore these points through two rather different case studies; namely Classical Athens and the Inca Empire. In both cases, my concern is to show how hegemony weaves political power into the material interdependencies of objects, identities, technologies and life-ways. For the sake of brevity and comparability, in both cases I will emphasise relational networks involving politics, gender, domestic groups, labour and a single category of material culture.

Articulating power in classical Athens

Perhaps the most famous discussion of the interdependency of politics, gender and labour is to be found in Aristotle's *The Politics*. Here, Aristotle designates the household (*oikos*) as the foundation of the Greek city-state (*polis*) and the foundation of the household as an '... association formed by men with these two, women and slaves ...' (Aristotle *The Politics* I.ii.1252b). Following his own analytical method, Aristotle breaks down the complex politics of the *polis* into its simplest constituent parts, and there finds a triad relating male citizens to women and slaves by means of the household. Aristotle's view that the *polis* could be built upwards from the relationships of the *oikos* (see Nagle 2006) is interesting since these reproductive relationships, based on dependency, labour and gender, are precisely what is excluded from the civic politics of the *polis* (see pp. 81–5). Hence, we will begin our exploration by considering the paradox of citizenship, slavery and gender in Classical Athens under the democracy (508–322 BC).

Polis, citizen, state?

In the vast literature on the *polis* as a political form, one frequent theme is the problematic relationship between ancient Greek understandings of the nature of the *polis* and modern understandings of the nature of the state. By *polis* I actually mean Classical Athens (508–322 BC), which was in fact an atypical *polis* in terms of its large population and far-reaching democratic institutions. It is, however, the Greek *polis* from which most of our surviving evidence originates and, it must be said, it is an interesting case to consider in it own right.

The *polis* of Athens incorporated both the city of Athens itself and the peninsula of Attica (Figure 4.1). For much of the period from Cleisthenes' democratic reforms in 508 BC until the dissolution of Athenian democracy by Antipater of Macedon in 322 BC, Athens was at least notionally governed directly by its male citizen body. The Assembly (*ekklesia*) ratified decrees proposed by the Council (*boule*), and its membership was open to all adult male citizens registered in one of the 139 municipalities (*demes*) into which Athens and Attica were divided (see Hansen 1991). Normally, 6,000 or more citizens would attend and vote at Assembly meetings. The Council acted as an executive body that drafted the agenda for the Assembly and consisted of 500 members chosen by lot for one year terms. Even with some councillors serving more than one term, Mogens Herman Hansen (1991: 249) estimates that in the fourth century BC one-third of all male citizens over eighteen years of age, and two-thirds of all male citizens over forty years of age served at least one term as a councillor. In other words, under the democracy the governmental apparatus of Athens was the entire body of male citizens.

Figure 4.1 Map of Classical Greece featuring the *polis* of Athens

For classic state theory, the governmental apparatus of Athens presents a problem in that, despite its scale, centralisation and evident agency, it is not distinguished from its citizen body. In the words of political theorist Justin Rosenberg, the *polis*

> ... does not have any existence other than the political self-organisation of the citizenry. It has no bureaucratic apparatus to which the decision-making authority of the populace is formally alienated and which might provide a basis of 'independent' interests and capacities. It is anything *but* autonomous in this restricted empirical sense. And yet it talks like a state! (Rosenberg 1994: 79)

While this 'problem' has been raised many times, for present purposes it will suffice to consider recent exchanges between Moshe Berent (2000; 2006) and several critics (Grinin 2004; van der Vliet 2005; Anderson 2009; *cf.* Miyazaki 2007), regarding his claim that Athens is best classified as a stateless society.

Berent follows Weber in understanding the state as that set of institutions holding a monopoly on the legitimate use of force in a given territory (Berent 2000: 258–60; *cf.* Weber 1978: 54). In other words, the state is specifically the sum total of the police, army, judiciary, and legislature, etc. ... distinct from the citizen body of a given territory. For Berent it is precisely this idea of institutions distinct from the citizen body that does not hold for Classical Athens. In particular, Berent notes two aspects of Classical Athens that render it a stateless society. The first is the distribution of the means of coercive force amongst the citizenry (esp. self-armed hoplite land-owners as a volunteer army), rather than its concentration in coercive apparatuses (i.e. the police or a standing army), and a concomitant reliance on volunteerism and 'self-help' in law enforcement and civil defence. The second is the lack of structural differentiation between ruler and ruled, in that most offices rotated annually between citizens drawn by lot.

Much of the exchange between Berent and his critics hinges on differing interpretations of the evidence and the initial definition of the state. For example, both Grinin (2004: 127) and van der Vliet

(2005: 128) argue that the troop of Scythian archers who were among the public slaves owned by the *polis* of Athens essentially acted as a police force. Berent (2006: 144), in contrast, argues that their role was limited to keeping order in defined contexts and they therefore did not constitute a police force in the sense of having a general responsibility for law enforcement.

Looking past these definitional debates we do learn some interesting things about Athens. As Virginia Hunter (1994) has shown, Berent is right to stress the limited nature of formal coercive apparatuses in Athens. However, what the *polis* did was sanction and legitimise the use of seemingly 'private' coercive force by means of legal decisions and legislative decrees (Hunter 1994: 188). Indeed, Edward Harris (2007) goes much further in emphasising the strict limits placed on 'self-help' in legal matters and the need for legitimation through judicial and legislative offices. Justifiable homicide (against robbers or adulterers caught *in flagrante*) in Athens was an interesting case of a private action that existed only through its public legitimation (Adam 2007). For example, Makoto Miyazaki (2007) argues that an Athenian citizen could legitimately exercise coercive force, but only if he could represent himself as an agent of public interest. He writes:

> … when Euphiletos, the speaker of Lysias 1 and cuckolded husband, killed Eratosthenes the adulterer of his wife, he claims that he said 'it is not I who am going to kill you, but the *nomos* of the polis, which you transgressed and had less respect for than your pleasure'. (Miyazaki 2007: 96)

Hence, the aggrieved husband portrays himself not as one exacting personal vengeance, but as one performing as an agent of the *polis*, enforcing its laws and acting in its interests. To use the terms we introduced in Chapter 1, the *polis* provided the 'principle of intelligibility' for the 'private' actions of citizens carried out as agents of public interest.

The *polis* as a virtual authority legitimising private action is paralleled by the role of the *polis* as the guarantor of private exchange relations through the minting and assaying of coins. For example, Athenian silver coins were tested and counterfeits removed from circulation by Athenian public slaves with the title *Dokimastes* ('tester'). In both cases, the guarantor of the value of a coin, or the legitimacy of a court ruling, may have been the political community, but it was a political community that had been hypostasized as a collective agent, capable of expressing a will, making decisions, and maintaining an historical presence across generations. This point is implied by Mogens Herman Hansen (1998) in arguing that the word *polis* could be used to refer to a transcendent public power in a manner not unlike current uses of the word 'state'. It is also argued explicitly by Gregory Anderson (2009), who contends that in Classical Athens *demos* ('people') could also refer to a hypostasized power with a collective will and not just the specific individuals constituting the Assembly of the *polis* at any given point in time.

One may protest that Hansen's and Anderson's respective interpretations of *polis* and *demos* as virtual entities underemphasize the fact that male citizens were actively conscious of constituting the *polis* and of being themselves the *demos*. Hence, Berent's argument that public power and the citizen body were never distinguished in Classical Athens. Be this as it may, one must accept that the citizen body of Athens was constituted as a virtual public power in other ways. As Mogens Herman Hansen writes:

> The *polis* was a society of *citizens*. It was a male society from which women were excluded; all foreigners were also excluded, and metics and slaves, though domiciled in the *polis*, were not members of it, a fact of which they were reminded every day of their lives, when the citizens went off on their own to deal with affairs of state in the Assembly or the Council or the courts. ... Yet every day, when the meetings to deal with affairs of state were over, citizen, metic and slave went off to work side-by-side as artisans, traders or farmers: in the economic sphere the stranger was a part of the society, though in the political sphere he was not. (Hansen 1991: 62)

Hence, the practice and ideology of citizenship was a foundation not just for self-government, but also for the governing of others who, outside of the political domain, constituted a significant component of a wider Athenian society (especially with regard to production, commerce, religion and education; see Cohen 2000). Interestingly, in so far as Athens could be said to have a non-elected civil service, it was largely constituted by public slaves and the female dominated priesthood of Athena. Hence, male citizenship was constructed by separating it from women, slaves and foreigners (*metics*) in two directions; first by limiting self-government to male citizens and then by separating self-governing male citizens from what might be anachronistically termed public-sector employment. This points to male citizen identity as the site of significant hegemonic activity: something that requires our closer attention.

Athenian citizenship was primarily acquired as a male birthright, initially through an Athenian father, but after 451 BC only when both parents were of Athenian birth. While wealth, status and ability varied considerably amongst citizen males, the political domain was defined by a notional equality between male citizens in terms of the ability and opportunity to participate in the political process: what Ian Morris (2000: 111, quoting Dahl 1989) calls the 'strong principle of equality'. This notional equality was embodied in a 'middling ideology' where the male citizen was made equal with his fellow citizens through their mutual autonomy, ideally with none rising too high, nor falling too low in relation to others (Morris 2000: 112–13). It is true that Athenian literature preserves what is often called an elite view (e.g. 'the Old Oligarch', Plato, Aristotle) that sought to divide or rank the citizen body according to wealth, occupation, ability or birth. Indeed, Athens did see short-lived coups to install an oligarchy on two occasions (411 BC and 404 BC) during the life of the democracy. However, this elite view does not seem to have ever formed an effective counter-hegemony to that of the middling citizen, and in many cases operated within, rather than against, the hegemony of Athenian citizenship.

The middling ideal of Athenian citizenship was embodied in the hoplite farmer-soldier, a citizen with enough land to support his household and to pay the costs of arming himself and participating in the Athenian army (Hanson 1995: 221–89). However, the citizen body was not limited to hoplites, including as it did extremely wealthy landowners as well as those who were relatively poor and of low status (e.g. *thetes*), such as artisans, shopkeepers and the landless. Furthermore, although slave ownership was also an ideal, held by Aristotle to be necessary for full participation in political life (*The Politics* III.v), not all Athenian citizens owned slaves. In effect, Athenian democracy was a fractious coalition of poor and rich citizens who occupied different positions in relation to the means of production (especially control of labour and land).

If we remember our discussion of Gramsci, we can see that Athenian citizenship was a form of hegemony. Essentially, it represented as universal the interests of a limited segment of society (native freemen) for the purposes of political rule, and it did so by the selective articulation of shared cultural resources, in this case the 'strong principal of equality' amongst others. However, in contrast with Gramsci's views, the hegemony of Athenian citizenship did not produce a political apparatus that was directly coterminous with class in the sense of only investing slave-owners or land-owners with political power (*cf.* Nafisi 2004). This does not mean that politics in Athens transcended class or wealth, indeed quite the opposite is true (Davies 1981; de Ste Croix 1981). However, it does highlight the fact that we cannot presume that political power is simply another name for class or wealth, and instead we must examine the historical dynamic of their articulation.

Free men and others

The apparent autonomy of the political domain in Athens was achieved by demarcating it very carefully; promoting notional equality by excluding as far as possible relations of dependency. Hence, the sharp contrasts between male citizens, Athenian women, slaves and foreigners (*metics*) that structured citizen identity. Under the hegemony of middling citizenship, relations of mutual and hierarchical dependency were represented as internal to the *oikos* (household), most obviously in the case of relations between husband, wife and children, but also in the relationship between master and slave. Note, for example, that even the largest mining ventures and craft workshops staffed by slaves were organised and understood as extensions of the household of the owner (Harris 2002). Less directly, resident foreigners were also dependent on citizen households in the sense that they could not own land, were required to pay a special tax, and were required by law to have a citizen sponsor.

The Athenian *polis* played little direct role in economic production, and limited its surplus extraction to very specific activities and segments of society. To a large extent, this was made possible by the tribute Athens extracted from the Delian League as its *de facto* empire, as well as the duties levied on the abundant trade running through Athens's port at Piraeus. However, economic production and *polis* revenues were also dependent on volunteerism and the 'private' actions of autonomous households, especially the wealthiest ones. A rich silver strike at the Laurion mines led to a rapid expansion of mining operations in the fifth century BC that generated considerable revenue for Athens. However, this revenue came in the form of lease agreements with individual citizens, who then organised a portion of the silver ore extraction and processing as an enterprise of their personal *oikos*, manned by their own slaves (Hooper 1953; 1968). Similar sources of revenue included the leasing of public land to (usually wealthy) households, and various tariffs associated with foreign trade.

Interestingly, direct extraction of surplus did occur in two contrasting cases. Resident foreigners (*metics*) were required to pay a regular head-tax that was a simple obligation to the *polis* with few implications beyond the generation of revenue. In contrast, the wealthiest citizens were expected to use their private resources to fund specific public projects (termed 'liturgies' by scholars) in the form of festivals, performances and especially the construction and manning of warships

(Davies 1981; Gabrielsen 1994). To some extent this 'privatised' many of the *polis*'s major expenditures and gave wealthy Athenians some latitude in terms of displaying wealth in a socially acceptable, and at times politically expedient, manner.

Despite the apparent autonomy of politics from production in Classical Athens, ancient authors were very much aware that the equality of male citizens, and hence Athenian democracy itself, was made possible by specific relations of production. Motivated by conflict between aristocratic landowners and the poor in the early sixth century BC, the Athenian legislator Solon is credited with admitting the poorest citizens into Athens's then oligarchic assembly, abolishing debt-bondage and reforming land tenure. While the historicity of Solon's specific reforms remains an open question (see Blok and Lardinois 2006), archaeological surveys do seem to register significant changes in settlement and land use in the form of dispersed farmsteads and more intensive farming practices by the time of Cleisthenes' democratic reforms in 508 BC (Bintliff 2006; Forsdyke 2006). In particular, the increased autonomy of poorer citizens that came with the elimination of debt-bondage and other forms of direct dependency (e.g. serfdom) correlates with a rapid increase in Athens's reliance on slave labour in the realm of production (Finley 1981; Jameson 1977/78).

Athenian literature of the fifth and fourth centuries BC suggests an aversion even to wage-labour on the part of Athenian citizens (Cohen 2002; but *cf.* Wood 1988: 137–44). Poor citizens might work as craftsmen or shopkeepers; however, this was generally organised as self-employment, in contrast to the large workshops owned by wealthy citizens and staffed with slaves (Harris 2002). Literary evidence suggests that, when forced to hire themselves out, poor citizens preferred poorly remunerated seasonal employment such as olive harvesting, as this did not involve continuous dependence on an employer (Burford 1993: 190–1). Publicly-funded payments for service as a rower in the Athenian navy, or for attendance at the Assembly, may have provided another means for the poorer citizens of Athens to avoid selling their labour directly to fellow citizens. Hence, for Classical Athens, it seems that democracy was made possible, at least in part, by the transfer of economic dependency from poor citizens to non-citizens; namely slaves and foreigners (*contra* Wood 1988; see Foxhall 2002; Jameson 1992). While the political apparatus of Classical Athens may have had a relative autonomy with regard to class, it was directly coterminous with gender. Athenian women had a certain status as members of citizen households destined to create further legitimate citizens (Osborne 1997), and as leading figures in interlinked rituals of the lifecycle and the agricultural cycle (Dillon 2002). However, in terms of the political life of the *polis*, women were excluded in that they were not permitted to vote or participate in the Assembly. Furthermore, in Athens there was a strongly gendered division of labour in social and biological reproduction, with appropriate female labour, sexuality and authority ideally defined and contained by the household.

Athenian literature and art frequently map gender onto a spatial contrast between domestic and civic domains; principally the house as the domain of women and the outdoors in general, and key civic spaces, such as the Assembly, the Agora or the gymnasium in particular, as the domain of men. In this literature, women operating outside of the domestic context, or men operating within it, often serve as exemplars of shame, humour or liminality, as in the case of forensic speeches regarding adultery, the role of the *hetairai* (highly cultured prostitutes), or Aristophanes' comedies premised on collective political action by Athenian women (e.g. *Lysistrata* or *Ecclesiazusae* = 'Women in the Assembly') (see Davidson 2011). As Lin Foxhall (1994) notes, this binary engendering of space in Athens was part of a masculinist ideology, rather than a straightforward description of the lives of Athenian women and men. This ideology stressed the formation of autonomous male citizens as heads of households (*kyrios*) through civic institutions and homoerotic relationships that drew young men away from their natal households. In doing so, this ideology ignored the obvious role of women as widowed mothers and new wives in forming these same 'autonomous' households across generations.

In reality, this engendering of domestic and civic domains was never a simple case of female oppression and housebound seclusion, as might be suggested by an uncritical reading of the literary sources. Within the *oikos* women both managed household resources held in common and had independent title to the portion they brought into marriage through their dowry (Foxhall 1989). Indeed, it was this merging of inheritances that made marriage and household formation key strategic elements in the perpetuation of names and property across generations. Outside of the house women maintained extensive social networks that entailed moving about the city on visits to the houses of other women (Taylor 2011). Women were also engaged in extra-household tasks that could require regular trips outside of the house, as in the case of filling water jugs at civic fountain-houses (Nevett 2011). In rural areas it is apparent that women on less well-to-do farms would, of necessity, have participated extensively in outdoor labour associated with agriculture (Scheidel 1995; 1996). Finally, citizen women did, on occasion, engage directly in extra-household commerce, selling goods in the Agora or taking on paid employment, although such cases were often seen as indicative of the poverty and ill fortune of the woman's household (Brock 1994).

Despite, or rather because of, its ideological nature, the representation of gender in Athens was a key site of hegemonic activity. As James Davidson notes:

> Whether or not this discourse of the real can be said accurately to reflect reality, it nevertheless represents a big, important fact in itself and one that is readily enmeshed with other central discourses concerned with Greek self-definition, class, politics and citizenship. (Davidson 2011: 608)

Importantly, this ideology allowed the male head of the household (*kyrios*) to be imagined as '... the individual empowered to cross the boundary between household and community' (Foxhall 1989: 31), representing the *oikos* in the *polis*. This in turn had implications, not only for the constitution of gender in Classical Athens, but also for the constitution of politics.

We can now return to Aristotle's paradox of the *polis* being constituted by domestic relationships (between men, women and slaves) that
were explicitly excluded from civic politics. Drawing a sharp divide
between civic and domestic spheres and mapping this to an equally
sharp divide between masculine and feminine identities allowed Athens
to be understood as a collection of households represented by their
male heads. The autonomy of these households allowed male citizens
to participate as notional equals in civic politics, without requiring the
direct redistribution of land or wealth. As we have seen, this autonomy
was achieved in part by limiting direct economic dependency between
citizen households. This in turn was facilitated by the employment of
slave labour (and foreign *metics*) by wealthy households engaged in
large-scale economic activities.

Houses for citizens?

As the preceding discussion suggests, houses constituted a material
setting of particular significance to Athenian citizenship, one that has
been of particular interests to archaeologists, and one that meshes well
with our present focus on gender and labour (Figure 4.2).

The transition from Early Iron Age Greek houses, with few internal
divisions and a clear reliance on exterior workspace, to the multi-
roomed Classical house with its internal courtyard has attracted
considerable scholarly attention (Coucouzeli 2007; Morris 2000: 280–6;
Nevett 2010a: 22–42). This attention has focused somewhat narrowly
on the timing of the transition, what it 'means' in terms of changing
social structures (i.e. the increased importance of the *oikos* relative to
larger kin structures), and what it 'represents' in terms of gender and
citizen ideologies.

In interpreting the courtyard house, archaeologists initially looked
for evidence of 'women's quarters' (*gunaikon*; Walker 1983), in keeping
with the long-standing, text-based view that Athenian women lived
in 'Oriental seclusion' from men along the lines of an Ottoman harem
(see Wagner-Hasel 2003). The existence of a rigid internal gender

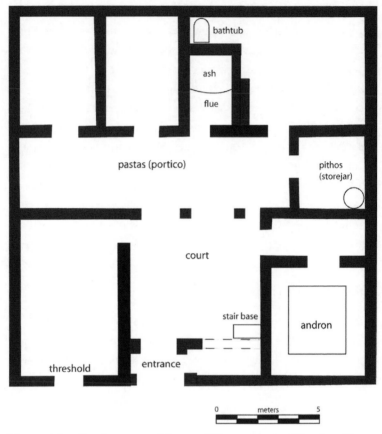

Figure 4.2   Greek courtyard house, fifth century BC, Olynthus House Avii4 (redrawn from Robinson and Graham 1938: Fig. 5)

division within Greek houses was soon questioned on textual (Cohen 1989) and archaeological (Jameson 1990) grounds. Instead, scholars drew on more nuanced interpretations of Islamic housing to argue that the key point of gender separation was between residents and guests, and hence between the inside and outside of the house (Nevett 1995). For example, figurative representations attest to female veiling outside the house, with the veil linked metaphorically to the 'protective' walls of the house in a variety of textual sources (Llewellyn-Jones 2007). As a key indicator of the division between resident and guest, Lisa Nevett (2010a: 43–62) points to the development of a special room, which she interprets as the *andron* ('men's quarter') of literary sources, used for symposia and to mediate the presence of male guests within the house. Identified by painted walls, mosaic floors, demarcated space for couches, an off-centred doorway to prevent lines of sight into other rooms of the house, and proximity to the main entrance, the *andron* is an identifiable feature of urban houses in Greece by the fifth century BC (Nevett 2010a: 55–6; Coucouzeli 2007 and Morris 2000: 280–6 date this development as early as the eighth century BC).

Both Nevett (2010b) and Westgate (2007) have noted that the Classical Greek courtyard house was intentionally oriented inwards, presenting a closed façade to the street. Its single entrance restricted access to the *andron*, where interaction with male guests was mediated, and to the internal courtyard in which domestic activities were shielded from view and through which most rooms in the house had to communicate. This was a space suited to the control of visual and physical interaction, especially between household members and outsiders. From the perspective of the male head of the *oikos* this facilitated the protection of household resources and the household's reputation, as well as the monitoring of female sexual activity within the *oikos*, ensuring legitimate heirs, future marriage alliances, and unencumbered slave labour. In short, according to both Nevett (2010b) and Westgate (2007), the courtyard house embodied and reinforced the citizen ideology of autonomous, self-sufficient households that could be represented in the political domain by their male citizen heads. What then are we to make of this connection between Greek houses and Greek politics?

One limitation of ideological approaches to Classical Greek houses is that they fail to account for houses as a site of articulation between politics, economics and identities except in terms of symbolic messages and social aspirations. In other words, politics occurs discursively and is reflected materially. Yet the autonomy of the Classical Athenian household was not just a symbol of appropriate gender relations; it was also the practical foundation of an economic unit of production and consumption. The household basis of labour relations (i.e. slavery and the gendered division of labour) and wealth accumulation are what allowed the emergence of wealth differences between citizens without the emergence of relations of dependency. These economic relations were learned and reinforced in the bodily experience of the house and household land-holdings. These experiences were embodied in terms of who moved freely as a member and whose movements were constrained as a guest, by why and in what manner household members crossed the threshold into the public domain, and by the actualities of creating, accumulating, managing and using household resources. In this sense the house was a key site for constituting, and not just materialising, the material interdependencies of economy, politics, gender and identity in Classical Athens. These material interdependencies are what was activated, reinforced and reinscribed through the practices of citizen hegemony. In this way, politics, labour, gender and domestic groups 'hung together' in a distinct way that was mediated by the physical form of the Classical courtyard house and the daily patterns of movement and interaction that this physical form afforded. In Latour's terms, the Classical courtyard house was an entity that did not sleep, creating associations that did not break down (Latour 2005: 70). The significance of this distinct 'spatio-temporal fix' (Jessop 2006) will be clearer if we turn to the very different case of the Inca Empire.

Labour, gender and power in the Inca Empire

Ruled by a divine king (*Sapa Inca*), geographically and demographically immense, possessing a centralised tribute economy lacking any standardised medium of exchange, and a social system based on gender complementarity (distinct, but equal, male/female roles), it would be hard to invent a polity more different from Classical Athens than the Inca Empire. Yet, much as in the case of Athens, political power in the Inca Empire required the articulation of distinct social

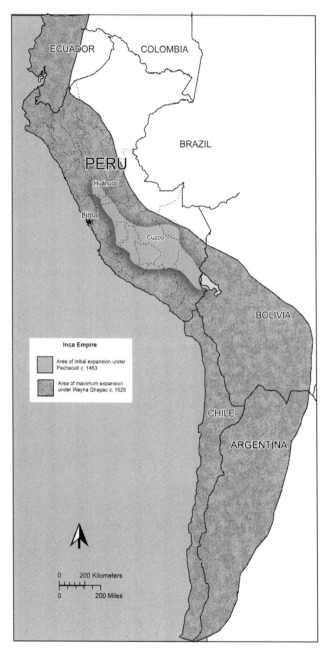

Figure 4.3 Map of the Inca Empire

fields, such as labour, production, gender and domestic groups. These articulations were multiple, but come together in a particularly striking way in a network centred on labour service, *chicha* (a beer made from masticated maize), and *acllacona* ('chosen women' who brewed *chicha* and wove textiles for the use of the Inca Empire).

The Inca Empire (Figure 4.3) both expanded and collapsed rather rapidly, although it was founded on a longer prehistory of state-formation that included the consolidation of distinct ethnic populations in the Cuzco Valley, Peru, and immediately adjacent regions (Bauer and Convey 2002). Much of what we know regarding the specific events of Inca imperial history depends upon accounts written by Spanish and indigenous authors in the century following Francisco Pizarro's kidnap and murder of Emperor Atawallpa in AD 1532. According to these chronicles, the Inca state entered its imperial phase of rapid expansion following Pachacuti Inca Yupanqui's usurpation of the throne and miraculous defeat of the invading armies of Chanca in AD 1438. Over the next 90 years the Inca Empire expanded along the Andes mountain range to incorporate over 2 million km^2 and perhaps between 6 and 14 million people (McEwan 2006: 93–6). On the death of the Emperor Wayna Qhapac (Spanish: Huayna Cápac) in 1528, a war of succession broke out between his sons Atawallpa and Wascar Inca, leaving the Inca Empire weakened and divided on the eve of the arrival of the Spanish.

The diversity of the Andes meant that the Inca Empire incorporated a patchwork of distinct ecological zones and ethnic groups. In integrating this diversity, Inca imperial policy encouraged standardisation, while allowing – even promoting – regional differences in specific domains (e.g. Wernke 2006). The key to Inca policy was something we have already seen in our discussion of hegemony and in other case studies, namely the selective appropriation, transformation and reinscription of shared practices and values (e.g. Jennings 2003; Silverblatt 1987). Here, the fact that the diverse ethnic groups of the Andes seem to have shared many practices, orientations and values with each other, and with the Inca, was strategically important to Inca imperialism.

One such shared practice was the pan-Andean tradition of labour service. Andean households were traditionally organised into extended groups called *ayllu* that combined kinship, bi-lateral inheritance and territory to form local communities. Households regularly contributed labour to assist fellow *ayllu* members or to undertake collective tasks of relevance to the community as a whole (Murra 1980: 90–2). In general, this labour service could take one of two forms. As delayed, symmetrical reciprocity, called *ayni*, shared labour implied equality, with participants continually creating and repaying the debt of mutual assistance over time (Flannery et al. 2009: 35–6, with references). As hierarchical, asymmetrical exchange, called *min'ka*, labour was recompensed immediately, usually with food and *chicha*, as in the case of work done for the *ayllu* head (*cuarac*) who then rewarded the labourers with a feast. Importantly, the *min'ka* arrangement implied lower status and dependency on the part of those giving labour and receiving food, distinguishing in this way between owning and working the land (Gose 2000: 86).

The Inca imposed a form of labour service on those they conquered (LeVine 1987; Murra 1980: 89–186), known as *mit'a* ('turn') in reference to the fact that each household took their 'turn' fulfilling the obligations placed upon higher-level groupings to which they belonged. Work included a wide variety of tasks, such as agricultural labour, weaving, brewing, construction, mining and warfare. Most labour service was carried out on specific projects by people based in their own communities. Under these circumstances, the Inca Empire cast itself in the role of host, providing food and *chicha*, as well as cloth and other material goods, to work parties during their period of service. As LeVine (1987: 15–17) notes, labour service could also require full-time work, sometimes away from home (e.g. mining, warfare), with communities rotating the obligation amongst their members and the Inca administration providing for the material needs of those in full-time service.

In contrast to this rotating labour service, the Inca Empire expropriated the labour of some of its subjects more continuously, thereby associating them with the Empire in a categorical manner (Murra 1980:

153–86). This included skilled specialists (*camayoc*) in various activities, such as craft production; colonists (*mitmaq*) moved wholesale to farm, populate or defend new territory for strategic reasons; retainers (*yanacona*) who were usually non-Inca elites assigned as servants to high-status Incas; and finally 'chosen women' (*acllacona*) who are of particular interest in this chapter.

Acllacona (sg. *aclla*) or 'chosen women' were young girls selected from amongst the Inca provinces for their beauty and deportment (see, for details of the Spanish accounts of *acllacona*: Alberti Manzanares 1986; Costin 1998; Gose 2000; Silverblatt 1987: 81–108; and Surette 2008: 14–66). Once selected, the girls were cloistered in an *acllawasi* (*wasi* = 'house'), where they were taught by senior 'chosen women' (*mamaconas*, 'esteemed mothers') to be highly skilled weavers and brewers of *chicha*, as well as knowledgeable attendants in state temples and shrines (Figure 4.4). Depending upon the status of their families they may have also been engaged in food preparation and agricultural work on the lands of temples and the Emperor (Surette 2008: 46–8). Conflicting ages for selection are given in the Spanish chronicles, but most suggest that the girls were prepubescent, and all stress the importance of virginity during their years of cloistering, often drawing parallels with Christian nuns. It does seem that sexual activity, and indeed most male contact, was strictly limited for *acllacona* as the Inca Empire asserted control over their reproductive potential. Girls of the highest status (e.g. members of the Inca royal family) were housed in the *acllawasi* of Cuzco, associated with the Temple of the Sun. Known as 'wives of the Sun', these *acllacona* wove cloth that was exclusive to the Inca Emperor and his Queen (the *Coya*). Lower status girls were housed in *acllawasi* in provincial centres and could be designated 'wives of the Inca'.

In being separated from their ethnic communities and assimilated to the governing apparatus of the Inca Empire, *acllacona* were elevated to a high status during their residence in the *acllawasi*. At the end of their residency *acllacona* seem to have had one of four fates: 1) most commonly they were given in marriage to soldiers, nobles or other

Figure 4.4 *Acllaconas* spinning wool within an *acllawasi* compound overseen by a *mamacona* (source: Poma de Ayla 1936 [1615]: 298)

officials as a sign of the Inca's esteem, usually, but not always, in their native province; 2) less commonly they became secondary wives or concubines of the Inca himself; 3) they remained in the *acllawasi* and assumed the role of *mamacona*, training and overseeing future generations of *acllacona*; or 4) they served as sacrificial offerings as part of the annual festival cycle and in response to extra-ordinary events (e.g. disease, natural disasters, military defeat). Upon their death, sacrificed *acllacona* became oracular deities (*huacas*), honoured and consulted in regional shrines.

Each of these four fates served to generate hierarchy and transfer it to the Inca Emperor through the assimilation of *acllacona* to the Inca state. According to the Spanish chroniclers, the Inca Emperor appropriated the right to allocate women in marriage throughout the Empire by requiring men to seek official sanction in order to wed. In this way, the Inca Emperor inserted himself into the superior role of 'wife-giver', and subsumed marriage and household formation to his Empire. Giving *acllacona* as brides to reward imperial service or cement an alliance was both an extension and an amplification of the Inca Emperor's 'wife-giver' status, fusing reproductive relations with empire building. The remaining three fates merged *acllacona* into the governing apparatus of the Empire even more fully, permanently alienating them from their natal communities except in the transformed role of living or deified intermediaries (Gose 2000: 88; Silverblatt 1987: 94–100).

My interest in the *acllacona* stems from the link they provide between *mit'a* labour service and the Inca Empire. First, as brewers, *acllacona* were central to the provisioning of workers with *chicha* as well as food on behalf of the Empire. How far down the social ladder and how far out into the provinces this extended is not clear. *Chicha* has long been a high-value food item in the Andes with ritual and political significance (Hastorf and Johanessen 1993; Jennings and Bowser 2009). This relates in part to the difficulties of growing maize at altitude and to the cultural and religious significance attached to intoxication. The brewing of *chicha* on a large-scale, as would occur in the case of large festivals and the feeding of work parties, is both time and labour intensive (Jennings 2004). As Jennings (2004: 252) notes, the labour cost of large-scale production can be reduced by using larger brewing pots (e.g. 170 litres versus 80 litres), and indeed one finds such large brewing pots on Late Horizon (Inca period) sites in the Andes. However, large pots are typically associated with centralised brewing, as their manufacture and movement stretches the labour capacities of women in individual households (Jennings and Chatfield 2009). At the same time, because *chicha* does not keep or transport well, it must be brewed near to the site of its consumption. Hence, the Inca Empire and its agents would have had need of large-scale brewing labour and facilities spread across the Empire in order to sponsor its feasting activities.

Spanish chronicles suggest that at its height the *acllawasi* in Cuzco housed 1,500 *acllacona*, while Pedro de Cieza de León, writing in 1553, mentions the former existence of *acllawasi* at 21 different locations, noting several as housing more than 200 women (Surette 2008: 37–8, 80–2). Pilar Alberti Manzanares (1986: 161) suggests that *acllawasi* were located in 28 primary population centres of the Empire, leading Flannery Surette (2008: 38) to estimate a total population of 6,900–15,500 *acllacona* at the height of the Inca Empire (1,500–2,000 for Cuzco and 200–500 for provincial centres). Hence, it seems reasonable to suggest that, at least in Cuzco and major provincial centres, *acllacona* were available to brew and serve *chicha* on behalf of the Inca Emperor on a scale commensurate with the needs of the *mit'a* system. However, Gose (2000: 87) thinks that *acllawasi* were even more widespread than this, citing evidence from the Spanish chronicles for the presence of *acllawasi* even in small settlements in order to suggest that *acllacona* provided most of the labour needed to brew and feed those doing *mit'a* service in all parts of the Empire.

Very few excavated structures have been identified as *acllawasi*, the best example of which is from the site of Huánuco Pampa, a provincial administrative centre built as a new settlement by the Inca, and located in Huánuco Department of modern Peru. To the north of the site's monumental plaza, excavators identified a walled compound built of fine-cut Inca masonry and measuring ca. 100m. x 140m. This compound had a single gated entrance and enclosed a plaza and 50 barrack-like rectangular buildings each measuring between ca. 65m² and 95m² (Morris and Thompson 1985: 70–1, Fig. 8). Within this compound excavators found spindle whorls and bone weaving implements (Morris and Thompson: 70, Pl. 42–3), as well as '[h]undreds if not thousands' of large jars believed to be for the brewing of *chicha* (Morris and Thompson 1985: 70). The restricted access, large-scale, repetitive housing, and dense artefactual evidence relating to weaving and, most particularly, brewing, all support the impression provided by the Spanish chronicles of *acllawasi* as distinct institutions capable of housing more than two hundred *acllacona*.

Further archaeological evidence points to the wider impact of Inca food provisioning. Scholars have identified a repertoire of Inca pottery based on forms and decorative motifs that appears as a distinctly foreign element in ceramic assemblages in Inca provinces outside of the Cuzco region. According to Tamara Bray (2003), the most widely distributed forms within this repertoire outside of the Cuzco region were the so-called *aríbalo*, a long-necked jar thought to be for the carrying and serving of *chicha*, the pedestalled cooking pot, used for boiling food, and the shallow plate, a basic serving vessel (Figure 4.5). Furthermore, Bray (2009: 119–21) notes that, in contrast to the Cuzco region, in the Inca provinces medium and large *aríbalos* dominate over small ones, suggesting that they were used primarily for consumption of *chicha* in larger groups.

While Andean communities maintained a mixed-farming regime throughout the period of the Inca Empire, there is some evidence that the significance of *chica* led to an increase in the cultivation of maize in areas conquered by the Inca (Hastorf 1990). Certainly, maize figured significantly in Inca tribute demands and was one of the key staples stored in the large-scale centralised storage facilities found throughout the Empire (see LeVine 1992). Maize also played a significant role in the ideology of Inca imperialism. The ploughing and the planting of maize were ritually linked to warfare as quintessential masculine activities.

Figure 4.5 Inca ceramic figurine of a man carrying an *aríbalo* of *chicha* on his back (photo credit: Werner Forman Archive/Museum für Volkerkunde, Berlin)

Indeed, the story of the original conquest of Cuzco at the dawn of Inca history included the introduction of maize by the founding Inca couple of Manco Capac and Mama Huaco, and was re-enacted annually by the Inca Emperor by breaking the earth to commence the ploughing and sowing season (Bauer 1996).

While I have focused primarily on their role as brewers, *acllacona* were also renowned as weavers of very fine cloth (see Costin 1998; Murra 1962; Surette 2008). Under the Inca, all households were required to produce cloth as tribute. These textiles were stored in central storage facilities across the Empire and distributed to soldiers and corvée labourers while they were doing service for the Emperor. However, *acllacona* wove much finer, more highly valued textiles using rarer materials such as the wool of the wild *vicuña* and, in the case of tunics for the Inca himself, even bat hair. Decorative patterns were distinguished by status and by ethnicity, making fine cloth garments quite literally markers of identity. At the same time, sumptuary laws made the distribution and possession of this fine cloth a central dynamic in the micro-politics of desire, favour and reward, bonding elite subjects to the Inca Emperor and his governmental apparatus.

Brewing and weaving were not, however, merely tools of imperialism made efficient and exclusive by the cloistering of *acllacona*. It has to be remembered that in the Inca Empire both brewing and weaving were women's labour par excellence. The gendered complementarity of work in the Andes meant that weaving and brewing were represented as female contributions to the collective enterprise of the household and the *ayllu*, just as agriculture and warfare were represented as male contributions. Hence, in the first instance, this was labour shared with, rather than extracted by, men (see Gose 2000; Silverblatt 1987: 3–39). Women's labour played a particularly important role in the feeding of work teams and in the provisioning and organisation of feasts. Hence, women's labour was key to both meeting the reciprocal responsibilities generated by *ayni* labour relations, and making possible the hierarchy-forming aspects of asymmetrical *min'ka* labour service through the provision of food and *chica* to teams of subordinate workers.

Irene Silverblatt (1987: 81–108) has argued that the Inca use of *acllacona* to appropriate female labour as a tool of imperialism was part of the transformation of a system of gender complementarity into a system of patriarchal hierarchy linked to class dominance (via conquest). Peter Gose (2000), however, has offered a more subtle view, arguing that the Inca Empire used *acllacona* to constitute itself in terms of both male and female modes of generating hierarchy. We have seen already how the *acllacona* played a role in defining the Inca Emperor as the ultimate 'wife-giver', a role in which junior males would carry out subordinate service to senior males in order to eventually be given a bride. Service to the Inca Emperor took a variety of forms, including agriculture, construction and warfare. However, all tribute to the Inca Emperor was cast as labour service through a legal fiction whereby the Inca claimed ownership of all of the resources of his domain (e.g. fish, maize, wood, etc.). Hence, in collecting tribute, the Inca Emperor was not represented as receiving goods, which would imply debt and subordination. Rather, he was represented as receiving in service the labour expended on extracting, making or raising resources that he already owned (Gose 2000: 85–6; Murra 1980: 29). Since the Inca Emperor sanctioned all marriages in the Empire, one means of interpreting tribute was therefore as bride service: labour given by a junior to a senior male in return for the right to marry (Gose 2000). At the same time, provisioning both tributaries and direct labourers with food and *chica* prepared by *acllacona* (as well as distributing the textiles these same women produced) meant that the Inca Empire could thereby also turn tribute into hierarchy-forming *min'ka* labour service, casting itself in the female roles of cook, brewer and weaver by means of its *acllacona* agents.

Already, prior to the formation of the Inca Empire, households, labour, gender and *chica* were related through a series of material interdependencies that had developed over many centuries (Hastorf and Johanessen 1993). These networks were particularly evident in local and regional politics (Gose 1993). By inserting himself into such networks as the ultimate 'wife-giver' and as the ultimate *min'ka* host, the Inca Emperor and his agents went a long way towards neutralising intermediary polities and articulating households, labour, gender and *chicha* directly with Inca imperial sovereignty. In Gose's words, under Inca imperial hegemony, household and state '... did not embody fundamentally different social principles or moralities. ... Rather, they were related as microcosm to macrocosm, in which the state appeared as a "generous" super-household of the senior generation, with abundant land and daughters to distribute to prospective sons-in-law' (Gose 2000: 93).

Summation

One of the most interesting contrasts between Inca imperial hegemony and the citizen hegemony of Classical Athens is the manner in which the former depended on the fusion of domestic and political domains as much as the latter depended upon their sharp distinction. In a checklist like Renfrew and Bahn's table this might appear as a problematic difference to be resolved, or as a culturally variable trait to be ignored. Yet, as we have seen, in each case these contrasting demarcations of domestic and political domains were central to the production and reproduction of sovereignty. In each case, relations of material dependency were assembled and made to work in the interests of sovereignty by means of practices, strategies and technologies that might be collectively labelled as hegemonic. We have seen that hegemony as an act of assembly, of making things 'hang together' in the interests of sovereignty, involves relational networks of material dependency between people and material culture, as well as modes of production, cultural practices, historical dispositions and inherited traditions. In the next chapter we will move on to explore more thoroughly the analysis of hegemonic practices, strategies and technologies.

5

Spectacle and routine

If France can be guided to peace and kept tranquil by shows, shows may in the end be as useful to them as Parliaments.

'Government by Shows – The Paris Fêtes', *Illustrated London News*, Saturday August 21, 1852 (Issue 5745): 138–9

Filling out forms, registering land, even paying taxes, might be considered the equivalents of sacrifice: little ritualised actions of propitiation by which one wins the autonomy to continue with one's life.

David Graeber (2007: 21)

Having discussed what we mean by sovereignty (Chapter 1) and hegemony (Chapters 2 and 3), as well as how all these things 'hang together' in given historical blocs (Chapter 4), I now want to turn our attention more directly to the question of the practices, strategies and relationships of sovereignty. If we are interested in analysing the practices of sovereignty in premodern contexts, we must first address a rather particular problem. As we noted in Chapter One, Michel Foucault defined governmentality as a specifically modern development; but what then are the distinctly premodern practices of governance? Looking closely, we find that on this point scholars divide.

As is often cited, Foucault himself characterised premodern society as a 'society of spectacle' where 'power was what was seen' (Foucault 1977: 187). Similar is Jürgen Habermas's (1989: 1–14) contrast between the development of a 'public sphere' in post-eighteenth-century Europe and what he terms the 'representative publicity' of medieval and absolutist Europe. According to Habermas (1989: 27–31), the public sphere is an imagined neutral space distinct from the private world of personal relationships and the political world of the state. It is a third space in which issues of public good can, in theory, be brought forward and rationally debated without reference to the identity of the protagonists. The development of a public sphere hinged on certain key developments of modernity, such as the idea of the state as a doubly impersonal institution that administered society (see Chapter 1) and the strict division of public and private domains encouraged by industrial capitalism. For Habermas (1989: 7–12), the public sphere contrasted with a premodern European society in which public good was derived from 'higher' principles (e.g. nobility, kinship, chivalry and, ultimately, divine authority) that embodied publicly in the speech and actions of a select group of elite representatives. Hence, Habermas implies that, in the case of premodern Europe, authority was dependent on its representation *before* the public rather than *by* the public (McCarthy 1989: xi)). In other words, it was dependent on spectacle.

The corollary of this focus on the visual nature of premodern authority is Anthony Giddens's (1985) claim that the ancient state was limited by its inability to penetrate the daily lives of its citizens. In James Scott's (1998: 2) words, '[t]he premodern state was … partially blind; it knew precious little about its subjects, their wealth, their landholdings and yields, their location, their very identity.' In other words, the necessity of visible power derived in part from the ancient state's inability to monitor and manage populations in their mundane activities and thereby shape political subjectivity in the manner of the modern state.

This view of premodern political authority as bound up in spectacle is reflected in the focus on display, monumentality and explicit, visible ideology in the archaeological analysis of premodern polities. Recognition of the importance of spectacle in premodern contexts cross-cuts otherwise opposing views regarding what spectacle does and why political authority exists. For example, both those who see public spectacle as promoting social solidarity and collective identification (e.g. Inomata 2006) and those who see it as a tool of elite manipulation (e.g. Demarrais et al. 1996) agree that the visual and aural experience of an explicit ideology was the primary means through which premodern political authority was constituted.

In contrast, scholars of so-called bureaucratic empires (e.g. Rome, the Inca Empire, Mesopotamia from at least the Early Dynastic III period, China from at least the Western Zhou Dynasty) often stress the elaborate and far-reaching measures employed by institutional agents within these polities in order to document, track and manage the daily minutiae of production, taxation and labour service (e.g. D'Altroy 1992; Eisenstadt 1963; Feng 2008; Steinkeller 1987). In such polities, temple and palace institutions seem to play a role in the management of everyday life that sits uncomfortably with the image of the ancient state as a thin veneer of spectacle.

Here we might contrast Foucault's society of spectacle with a society of routine in which political authority is manifest through its ability to structure, organise and manage various aspects of everyday life. If spectacle is power made visible through representation, then routine is power made invisible through regularisation. A concern for routine is evident in managerial (Wright 1977) and rational choice (Blanton and Faragher 2008) approaches to the early state, where the provision and administration of 'public goods', such as subsistence security or judicial mediation, is held to both justify and necessitate the existence of the state. However, one also finds an emphasis on the routine manifestations of political authority in practice-based approaches, which emphasise the spatial and temporal structuring of daily life for political ends through practical means such as building projects or landscape modification (Monroe 2010).

Ultimately, the choice between spectacle and routine is a false one, as there is a continuum of practices between these two extremes that are manifest to different degrees in different polities and different historical contexts. However, it is not enough to simply say that the practices of sovereignty in premodern polities can be placed along a continuum defined by spectacle and routine. In this chapter I hope to go further and show that spectacle and routine are not independent kinds of practices but are, in the end, directly linked through the medium of social performance.

Performance and social reproduction

The terms 'performance' and 'performative' have been widely used in archaeological literature (e.g. Joyce 2005). Yet, despite this ubiquity, the precise implications of a performative orientation for archaeological interpretation remain ambiguous and contested, especially when one turns to the analysis of political relationships. As Takeshi Inomata and Lawrence Coban note (2006: 12–16), social theorists have employed the concept of performance to analyse embodied human practice all along the continuum from spectacle to routine; taking us from the structured artifice of formal theatre to the performative utterances of everyday speech. In sketching an 'archaeology of performance', Inomata and Coban (2006: 16) prioritise scale and context in marking off spectacles as community-oriented and community-forming performances worthy of special attention for their potential as collective political acts. Ian Hodder (2006: 81–3), in contrast, rejects the very idea of distinguishing spectacle from routine, especially on the basis of its public context, scale or purported political efficacy. For Hodder, the structured patterns of movement, activity, decoration and burial attested (and constrained) by houses at Neolithic Çatal Höyük indicate a regulating of the residents' bodies that was no less performative or political than the public rituals of ancient kingdoms (Hodder 2006: 83). For Hodder, spectacle is simply 'a showing and a looking' (Hodder 2006: 82) and performance is 'a dimension of action that bridges to meaning and communication' (Hodder 2006: 85).

Hodder's argument is problematic in that spectacles are not merely 'a showing and a looking', but also a 'doing'. This involves human bodies/beings directly. Hence, the markedness of spectacles in terms of scale, place and sensorial intensity makes a difference to their effects;

to how they are experienced and to how they reference and orient relations between human bodies/beings (Houston 2006: 135–9; Kus 1992). The point is not to construct a typology of practices that divide the continuum from routine to spectacle, but to recognise that when embodied practice is formed and performed with different content, in different contexts, at different scales and with different degrees of markedness, it makes a difference to its effects and to its point of reference. Even the apparently repetitious world of Neolithic Çatal Höyük was punctuated by less regular events, such large-scale feasts (Hodder 2005) and perhaps even off-site rituals of a collective nature remembered in the murals and curated fauna for which the site's houses are duly famous (Hodder 2006: 85–7).

Hodder is correct to emphasise continuity in the performative nature of both spectacle and routine, in the sense of habituating bodily practices. Indeed, this continuity is the central organising principle of Paul Connerton's influential book *How societies remember* (Connerton 1989). Connerton is interested in the transmission of memory as a shared and social phenomenon. He focuses on what he calls habit memory as bodily skills and dispositions that are cultural, in that they must be learned from others (e.g. walking, playing the piano, bowing, waving good-bye), but which are performed habitually and in a manner that is not wholly dependent on symbolic representation. Connerton organises his text in a manner analogous to my use of spectacle and routine, examining two extremes through the categories of commemorative ceremonies and bodily practices. Connerton shows that, in the case of both commemorative ceremonies and bodily practices, habit memory forms an important substrate linking the formation and transmission of collective memory in any society.

Less clear is precisely what is being remembered when bodies are culturally constituted through habit memory. Certainly, collective memory includes symbolic representation through the memorialisation of specific events, and the repetition of narratives that convey shared concepts of identity and of social and cosmological order. However, Connerton includes much more than this in his attention to what he terms 'incorporating practices' (Connerton 1989: 72–3). By incorporating practices, Connerton refers to information transmitted intentionally or unintentionally by the bodily activity of one person in the presence of another, as in the case of smiling or conversing. He contrasts this with 'inscribing practices', such as writing or drawing, where information can be stored and transmitted in the absence of the author. As Connerton (1989: 78–9) admits, there are problems with treating inscribing and incorporating practices as two mutually exclusive and exhaustive categories of transmission practices, something that becomes clear when we introduce material culture into the mix (see pp. 106–7). However, as is evident from even a moment's reflection on what is incorporated by the category of incorporating practices, Connerton is concerned with social memory, not simply as the remembrance of things past, but rather as social reproduction itself: the memory of how to live in the world in a particular way.

The significance of this view of social memory becomes more clear if we consider the role of material culture in social memory so conceived. Andrew Jones (2007) has considered the place of material culture in the constitution of social memory as an embodied practice. Jones does this by means of C. S. Peirce's tripartite classification of signs, focusing in particular on material culture as an index (Peirce 1931: 531). An index is a sign that conveys meaning as a product of its close association with what it is signifying, as in the truism 'smoke means fire' (Peirce 1931: 531). Indices, in this sense, are not necessarily fixed in nature, but can both accrue and recede over time and place by means of material associations (hence, in the early twentieth century it was also said in some quarters that 'smoke means progress').

Elsewhere (Routledge 2004: 154–5) I have discussed 'kingly things' in the Iron Age Levant as indices of kingship in explicitly representational terms, that is to say as material culture that called kingship to mind via its associations with royalty. However, Jones's focus on embodied memory opens up some new possibilities in terms of understanding material culture as indices that 'call to body' as much as they 'call to mind'. As Jones (2007: 53) points out, material culture can involve inscribing practices in Connerton's sense of transmitting information in an objectified (disembodied) form, but material culture is also physically engaged with and hence can involve incorporating practices as well. These incorporating practices may elicit what Connerton (1989: 22–3) terms personal and cognitive memories (i.e. explicitly representational memories), due to the indexical associations of the material culture with past contexts and practices. However, physical engagement will almost certainly also elicit Connerton's habit-memory, in Heidegger's sense of the 'readiness-to-hand' of objects (Heidegger 1962: 95–101). Engagement with material culture elicits habit memory in how to deploy tools, how to move through space, how to comport oneself, where to look, and when to speak. Equally, engagement with material culture could fail to elicit such habit memory, highlighting one's foreignness, lack of knowledge, awkwardness, displacement, etc. Instinctively knowing which fork to use for your salad at a formal dinner implies much more than the immediate mechanical process of eating.

Embodied experience is performed in different contexts with different implications for social reproduction; implications that are resident in both symbolic representation and bodily dispositions. If social reproduction is the memory of how to live in the world in a particular way, realised across different contexts with different implications, then hegemony is the attempt to link these contexts together and thereby shape what is and is not remembered in the name of certain interests and not others. In the cases that interest us, sovereignty is part of what hegemony remembers: the transcendent nature of political apparatuses, their necessity, legitimacy and authority in key domains, and their relation to relations of force. The question is how is political authority remembered?

Let us begin with spectacle as the site most frequently linked to the reproduction of political authority in premodern polities. What does spectacle do, and wherein lies its political efficacy? Clifford Geertz (1980: 121–36) has famously argued against the idea that public spectacle can be analysed as a kind of false consciousness; a bit of sugar to coat the bitter pill of power. According to Geertz, Western political theory has, since the sixteenth century, remained wedded to 'the great simple' (Geertz 1980: 134) that politics is ultimately only about power in the form of coercion, violence, domination and mastery. For Geertz the reduction of symbolic representation to a political instrument, one that masks, obscures or ameliorates the real workings of power, cannot make sense of the 'theatre state' of nineteenth-century Bali, where '[p]ower served pomp, not pomp power' (Geertz 1980: 13). According to Geertz, what mattered in Balinese royal ritual was the constitution and reproduction of a coherent view of reality, with the king as the exemplary centre holding together an orderly social hierarchy, one that arguably did not exist separate from these ritual contexts.

Geertz's central critique is an important one. The cultural poetics of any public performance are its central intent and any interpretation that ignores this fact in the interest of uncovering what is going on 'behind the mask' of ritual will be a misinterpretation. At the same time, Geertz simply inverts the equation that he critiques, turning a mere mask into a mere masque. Geertz's insistence that the symbolic coherence of royal rituals resides at a level wholly distinct from the political reality of daily life means that in the end he provides us with no means of understanding either why state rituals took the particular form that they did, or why they should have proved compelling, efficacious or necessary (Bloch 1987: 294–7).

As an alternative, Inomata and Coben are keen to shift our analytical focus away from examining public performances as a 'closed system of their own aesthetics' (Inomata and Coben 2006: 17) in order to understand spectacle as a distinct kind of cultural performance. Spectacle, in these terms, is a cultural performance whose political effects, such as communal integration or mass communication, might be said to reside to a large extent in the scale and sensorial markedness of the event. Treating spectacle as a cross-cultural category grounded in a common human body raises difficult questions regarding the universality of sensorial (and somatic) experience (*cf.* Joyce 2005; Moore 2006). Yet these difficulties are not so problematic if one frames the category of spectacle historically; sensorially marked events may not have collective political effects of necessity, but they have certainly had such effects at many times and places in many different cultural contexts. Acknowledging the sensorial impact of spectacle does not, however, take us very far. It does not, for example, explain the intellectual activity surrounding the content of spectacles, nor does it explain their diversity or culturally specific efficacy.

Both Adam Smith and Susan Kus and Victor Raharijaona recognise this problem directly in relation to the political efficacy of Urartian figurative representations of ritual spectacles (Smith 2006) and Merina royal public discourse (Kus and Raharijaona 2006). For Smith (2006: 126), 'to attempt to understand political spectacle without an understanding of the visions that not only strike the eye, but stir the imagination, would seem to miss something fundamental about the phenomenon'. Similarly, Kus and Raharijaona conclude that if 'we come to understand that a sensorial ethos is implicated in any alternative way of being in the world, then we are challenged to come to understand the "how" of the *specific* materials used to create and sustain the political …' (Kus and Raharijaona 2006: 323). This recognition that the content of public spectacle was meaningful and appealing to specific people in a specific context brings us back to our discussion of hegemony.

In Chapter Two we saw how hegemony hinged on the selective articulation and transformation of cultural resources that rang true because of their generation in the realm of common sense (i.e. day-to-day existence). Both Smith and Kus and Raharijaona explain the political efficacy of performance in their case studies in a similar manner. Smith (2006: 126-7) argues that the bountious offerings of produce and animals carried by processions of worshippers in Urartian figurative art were a key to the political efficacy of these images, as abundance in the practical realm of daily production was harmoniously united with consumption in the cosmological realm of deities. Kus and Raharijaona point out how the naming of places, rhetorical performances and movement between and within places were inseparable components of royal public discourse in the early Merina state, playing on local values that viewed speech, memory and landscape as continuous with one another.

Hegemony resides in the constitution of a moral order and a coherent view of reality, much as in the case of the idealised patterns standing at the centre of Geertz's cultural analysis. Yet, as I have argued, this order is selectively constituted by articulating elements relevant to some experiences while excluding those relevant to others. In other words, one need not, indeed one cannot, choose between cultural poetics and political efficacy as each is embedded within the other. A coherent view of the world by definition excludes the incoherence of social and economic asymmetry, resistance and disenchantment.

If ritual performance is aimed at constituting or reproducing a moral order, and addressed to a hegemonic view of reality, questions of audience and intention become less pressing than when political efficacy is seen to reside strictly in the conveyance of a compelling message from ruler to ruled. Ritual performance can be addressed to a broad or restricted audience, to the performers themselves, to the gods, to past ancestors or to future descendants. What matters is that spectacle participates in, and thereby embeds its participants in, the construction and reproduction of a particular moral order.

This said, we have still not addressed the specific question of political authority. Public spectacle occurs in communities of very different sizes with very different political structures. It is not, therefore, the exclusive domain of centralised and transcendent political apparatuses. Rather than spectacle having the function of producing/reproducing political authority, it seems much more the case that political authority must inscribe itself onto (i.e. entrain) public spectacle in order to be reproduced.

It is interesting that in the case of both Urartu and Imerina one is dealing not only with public events, but also with the marking and memorialisation of these events in enduring media (e.g. stone) under the direction and sponsorship of a political apparatus. In the case of Urartu, Smith (2006) is dealing exclusively with representations of spectacle. As with much royal art, these representations have a generic quality that need not refer only to specific past events, and indeed may not refer to any specific event. Generic banquet scenes, processions of tribute and pious offering scenes can provide models or summations of spectacle in which actual spectacles participate and to which actual spectacles aspire.

Even when representing specific places and events, the memorialisation of spectacle can shape and transform those places and events. Ömür Harmansah (2007), for example, provides an extended discussion of expeditions to the 'source of the Tigris' at Birkleyn in eastern Turkey by Neo-Assyrian kings, and their commemoration of these expeditions in reliefs and inscriptions both at the cave of the water source itself (Dibni Su) and back home in various Assyrian cities. The source of the Tigris was already a significant place within the imaginative landscape of Assyria, since most of the Assyrian heartland was situated along, and dependent on, the Tigris River and its major tributaries. Harmansah (2007: 181–4) suggests that the inscribing practices of Assyrian kings transformed this already significant site by incorporating it into the rhetoric of Assyrian kingship. The continual inscription of Assyrian monuments at the source of the Tigris, and at home, transformed it into a 'site of memory'. In the imaginative landscape of Assyria the source of the Tigris became a place tied to the king himself through the actual (via expeditions), and virtual (via their representation) spectacle of his transcendent body projected outwards to sacred and significant places on the edges of the empire (Harmansah 2007: 195).

Inscribing practices seek to commemorate and fix spectacle in particular ways. They also transform the places of spectacle, and inscribe political authority on spaces in a manner that begins to move us along the continuum of performance away from spectacle and towards routine. As in the case of Shang oracle bones, spectacles become entrained as indices of political authority. For example, like so many of the royal rituals of Imerina, the erection of stones to commemorate collective agreements and significant foundational acts was not so much a practice invented by royalty as one appropriated, and thereby transformed, by royalty. Indeed, monolithic stones, erected to commemorate founding treaties or the ancestral tombs that define villages remain focal points for communal gatherings, judicial procedures and collective ritual to this day in highland Madagascar (e.g. Graeber 2007: 69–72; Kus and Raharijaona 1998). In the nineteenth century, under the monarchy, when agreements were reached a stone was erected and each party paid a tax in silver (*hasina*) to the monarch (Graeber 2007: 408n. 26). In this way the monarch became the guarantor of the agreement and was associated with the stone, which thereafter persisted as a feature of the landscape of a given village or field.

To summarise, when considering the techniques of sovereignty in premodern contexts, our choice is not really between societies of spectacle and societies of routine. Certainly, the degree to which techniques of sovereignty are encountered in the context of one's daily routine will vary considerably between polities and historical contexts. Some polities track their citizens closely and others seem to exist only in flurries of pomp and circumstance. However, in all cases we are dealing with social performances that involve both symbolic representation and habit memory; both callings to mind and callings to body, as it were. What matters is that the disparate contexts in which people remember, or are forcibly reminded of the place of political authority in their world are linked by reference to a coherent hegemonic order.

We can, therefore, define three points on the continuum from spectacle to routine. The first is the production of objects of direct intellectual reflection. These are the messages of utility and pleasure, of morality and public good, or of intimidation and fear, communicated through speeches, texts, images, performances, and built environments, amongst other means. These explicit spectacles serve to communicate messages of political authority. However, they also serve to regularise and routinise that authority through habitual bodily participation (e.g. as the audience for commemorative ceremonies), through the creation of settings and backgrounds (e.g. plazas, monuments and temples), and through the entrainment of media, contexts, objects and even time (e.g. festivals and calendrical observances) via their hegemonic associations. This routinisation of spectacle is the second point on our continuum and provides a bridge to the third: those more mundane techniques of sovereignty, such as the enumeration, taxation and regulation of subjects, more commonly considered as the routine manifestations of political authority.

What is interesting about these three points on the continuum from spectacle to routine is how often they prove to be inseparable in any given moment of social performance. Most particularly, spectacle and routine do not divide between ideological and practical activities. Praying and eating are both constituted in equal measure by elements of symbolic representation and habit memory. The interpretive significance of this fact will become clearer by briefly considering the relationship between ritual and water management in Classic Maya polities.

Royalty, routines and rituals: The place of water in Classic Mayan polities

Mayanists have shown a strong interest in the archaeology of performance (e.g. Houston 2006; Inomata 2006), and, honestly, who can blame them. Classic-period Mayan centres were structured around a core of built forms, such as plazas, stepped temple platforms, ball courts and inscribed stele, which seem oriented to facilitating and representing ritual events. By the Classic period (AD 250–900), the interaction of built spaces and images was highly developed, linking Mayan cosmology and local rulers in the context of collective festivals and ritual enactments of varying scales and levels of exclusivity (Sanchez 2005). Stele positioned around plazas and reliefs carved on building facades and stairways (along with polychrome vessels and wall paintings) depict deities, mythological figures, rulers and sacrificial victims, as well as dancers and other ritual performers (Houston 2006; Inomata 2006; Schele and Miller 1986). This emphasis on

Figure 5.1　Map of the Classic Maya heartland with sites mentioned in text marked

royal-sponsored festivals and public ritual evident in Classic Mayan centres fits with a model of Mayan polities as weakly bounded and radiating outwards from rulers who compete to control lesser rulers and a dispersed rural population with shifting, or cross-cutting, allegiances (e.g. Inomata 2004).

The built environment of most Classic Mayan centres also included sophisticated and extensive systems aimed at harvesting (Scarborough and Gallopin 1991), spreading (Dunning and Beach 1994), or controlling (Davis-Salazar 2006; French et al. 2006) the flow of water. While sub-tropical to tropical in terms of vegetation and rainfall, precipitation in the Maya heartland is highly seasonal, with a marked dry season from January to May. Approximately 70 per cent of the Maya territory (i.e. Petén and the Yucatán) is a lowland limestone shelf, creating a classic karstic environment where access to surface water is limited but subterranean water is abundant (Veni 1990). Much of the remaining Maya territory is made up of volcanic highlands and foothills, where watercourses are more abundant, but deeply incised or subject to seasonal flooding. Hence, water was available to the Maya, but only at certain times and places, and in a manner that required knowledge and favoured active management (Figure 5.1).

Not surprisingly, water is also one of the core elements in Mayan cosmology, imagery and ritual (Brady and Ashmore 1999; Fash 2005). For the Maya, water provided the link between terrestrial, celestial and subterranean worlds, most notably in the form of mountains on one hand and caves, springs and sink-holes (cenotes) on the other (Brady and Ashmore 1999; Vogt and Stuart 2005). Water glyphs, and water-related imagery such as water-lilies, were widely used on stele and architectural reliefs (Fash 2005; Schele and Miller 1986; see Figure 5.2). Similarly common was imagery associated with caves and mountains, widely viewed as the abode of the rain god Chaak and sources of both ground water and rainfall (Adams and Brady 2005; Brady 1997; Vogt and Stuart 2005). At a number of sites, including Chichén Itzá, Copán and Dos Pilas (Brady 1997; Brady and Ashmore 1999, Davis-Salazar

Figure 5.2   Si(j)yaj K'in Chaak II impersonating the water-lily serpent. Machaquilá Stele 4 (source: Photo by Linda Schele. Reproduced by permission of the Foundation for the Advancement of Mesoamerican Studies Inc.)

2003), the public architecture seems to have been laid out to incorporate, or align with, a cave or spring.

Caves, springs and cenotes, all subsumed under the word *ch'een* in Mayan hieroglyphs (Vogt and Stuart 2005: 157–63), are clearly associated with central institutions of political power in Classic Mayan polities. Most famous is probably the so-called 'Cenote of Sacrifice' at Chichén Itzá, where votive offerings of gold, jade, pottery censers and imported goods, as well as some human victims, were deposited in large numbers from the Late Classic through Post-Classic periods (Coggins and Shane 1984). However, royal (or a least elite) ritual use of caves can also be seen in many other contexts, such as the murals and glyphs from Naj Tunich cave complex in the Petén district of Guatemala (Stone 1995). At the same time, as is the case amongst recent Mayan communities (Adams and Brady 2005; Vogt and Stuart 2005), archaeological evidence suggests that the ritual use of caves extended beyond strictly elite practices and prior to the Classic period (Brady and Prufer 2005).

In general, ethnographies, especially the work of Evon Vogt (1969) in highland Chiapas, have documented the important role of small-scale, water related ritual in the everyday life of recent Mayan communities. Archaeological evidence suggests that such small-scale water related rituals, especially those associated with springs and caves, may have played a similar role in the daily life of ancient Mayan 'commoners' in the lowlands. Such rituals were therefore available for appropriation and transformation by elites in the Classic period for the hegemonic purposes of royal display (Davis-Salazar 2003; Lucero 2006; Scarborough 1998).

A number of scholars have linked these two aspects of water, arguing that water management and water rituals interacted to constitute and legitimise the authority of Mayan rulers. The control of water and the control of people is an equation that has been made frequently by scholars over a very long period of time, most famously by Karl Wittfogel in his book *Oriental Despotism* (1957). The position of the Maya in the 'irrigation management = despotism' argument has always been ambiguous, as such arguments focused on large-scale riverine irrigation, a technology that is generally unsuited to the karstic lowlands and incised volcanic highlands of the Mayan homeland. In the case of the Maya, the emphasis has not been on the administration of water canals for the purposes of irrigation, so much as on the management of still-water reserves during the dry season.

In mapping water catchments and reservoirs at a number of Mayan centres, most notably Tikal, Vernon Scarborough (1998; 2003: 108–15; Scarborough and Gallopin 1991) has argued that in the Classic period Maya rulers created large convex watersheds that captured and stored run-off rain water (Figure 5.3). This was achieved by building urban centres on elevated ground, using watertight masonry, and channelling run-off water downhill from core architectural complexes into large built, or modified natural reservoirs. Scarborough and Gallopin (1991: 659) define three kinds of reservoirs in Maya centres: 1) central precinct reservoirs, located in the settlement epicentre adjacent to the primary plazas and public architecture; 2) residential reservoirs, adjacent to residential neighbourhoods; and 3) *bajo*-margin reservoirs. The last of these reservoir types were located on the outskirts of sites adjacent to *bajos*, which are wetlands created by surface depressions in the limestone bedrock of the lowlands (Dunning et al. 2006). The degree to which ancient Mayan farmers modified *bajos* for the purposes of intensive agriculture (e.g. raised fields) is a point of some controversy; however, at the very least the margins of *bajos* formed important agricultural land in many parts of the lowlands (Dunning et al. 2006). Central precinct reservoirs usually had the largest storage capacity and were most closely associated with water symbolism and elite ritual performance. They were also connected by a combination of canals and topography to *bajo*-margins in such a way as to either recharge *bajo*-margin reservoirs in the dry season or to directly irrigate *bajo*-margin fields (Scarborough and Gallopin 1991: 360). Hence, as the name suggests, central precinct reservoirs played a central role in concentrating and providing both potable water and irrigation water during the dry season.

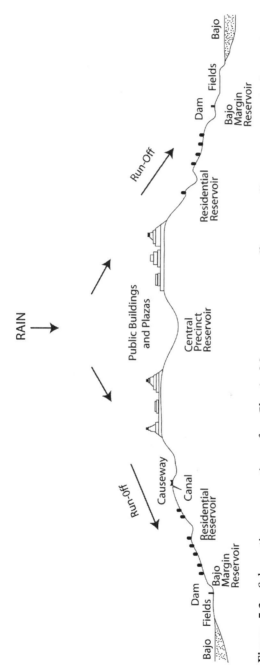

Figure 5.3 Schematic cross-section of a Classic Maya convex run-off water collection system (redrawn from Scarborough 1998: Figure 2)

Scarborough (1998: 136–7) notes that these water management systems concentrated water in a quantity and quality that otherwise would not exist and in a manner that allowed for its control by resident elites. Yet, according to Scarborough, the dispersed nature of Mayan settlement and land-use left rural sustaining populations with alternatives to dependence on elite controlled reservoirs and hence people had to be drawn into urban centres. To this end, Mayan rulers appropriated and elaborated water-related rituals that were centrally important to the world-view and social reproduction of the Maya.

For Scarborough (1998: 149), Mayan centres, in which the run-off water from temple platforms and plazas filled reservoirs, were understood as 'water mountains': man-made versions of the mountains from whose caves and springs both watercourses and rain clouds were said to emanate. For example, Scarborough points to the depiction of mountains composed of flowing water in the Tlalocan mural at the central Mexican site of Teotihuacan, and to the fact that *altepetl*, the Nahuatl (Aztec) word for village or community, translates as 'mountain of water'. By recreating a key site in the ideological landscape of Mesoamerica, one that produced a stable supply of water like its counterpart in nature, and then leading key rituals central to reproducing those supplies of water over time, Mayan rulers inserted themselves into the very centre of the universe.

Scarborough's version of the 'water = power' argument is what we might term the moderate version. He accepts, for example, that Mayan rulers could never fully monopolise water management in local communities (Scarborough 2003: 113). Scarborough also remains equivocal regarding the extent to which elite power was primarily founded on the control of water, and the extent to which dispersed settlements were dependent on centralised reservoirs during the dry season.

Such equivocation is not found in what might be termed the extreme version of the 'water = power' argument put forward most forcefully by Lisa Lucero (2006). Lucero's argument largely parallels Scarborough's, in that she argues that Mayan rulers collected and concentrated still-water reserves and that they drew dependents to urban centres and legitimized their control of still-water reserves by appropriating and elaborating key rituals. However, Lucero goes much further in terms of specifying the nature and mechanics of the relationship between Mayan rulers and Mayan commoners.

Lucero argues that broad categories of Mayan polities (i.e. minor centres, secondary centres and regional centres) correlate directly with the form and extent of centralised water management within those polities. In essence, she argues that the degree to which Mayan elites were able to extract surplus from Mayan commoners was directly correlated with the degree to which Mayan commoners were dependent on elite controlled still-water reserves during the dry season. Like Scarborough, Lucero gives a large role to ritual performance, seeing it as necessary to drawing people into major centres and placing Mayan rulers at the heart of key activities for reproducing the Mayan world (e.g. water purification and renewal). Yet, despite the attention she gives to ritual, in the final analysis ritual performance still functions primarily as a legitimising false consciousness in Lucero's argument. Power, which she defines principally as the ability to extract surplus, resides in the practical dependence of commoners on elite-controlled water.

The limits of Lucero's mechanistic view of the 'water = power' equation become evident when we begin to look beyond major lowland sites with large-scale reservoirs such as Tikal. For Lucero, the presence or absence of large regional centres is negatively correlated with the availability of dry-season water sources. Local centres, such as Saturday Creek in central Belize, do not develop into large centres because elites could not control the dispersed year-round water sources available to farmers (Lucero 2006: 72–3). As Kevin Johnston (2004) has pointed out, this ignores the evidence for household wells, and hence water self-sufficiency, found amongst small dispersed sites in the lowlands. Lucero (2006: 37) states that such wells are found in territories where regional centres did not develop, but this ignores Johnston's larger point that wells are difficult to identify at small rural sites and the ones that are known may only be the tip of the iceberg.

Whether or not Johnston is correct, Lucero's arguments seem to run into trouble when we look beyond the lowlands and consider regional centres in well-watered piedmont and riverine zones. At Copán, in western Honduras, a large regional centre of the Classic Maya period developed in the water-rich Copán valley. Amongst the more prominent water management features of this site are the conduits, drains and causeways that provide drainage and flood control for the principal architectural group and elite residential clusters of Copán (Davis-Salazar 2006). Also prominent are the artificially modified lagoons that serve as stable freshwater sources and are the focal point of a number of residential clusters in and around Copán (Davis-Salazar 2003). As Barbara Fash (2005; Fash and Davis-Salazar 2006; Davis-Salazar 2003) has pointed out, the lagoons in particular are associated with both water and royal, or elite, iconography such as water-lily headdresses, *tuun* glyphs and half-quatrefoil frames (both symbols of water-bearing caves). Fash and Davis-Salazar (2006) have suggested that these water-hole groups may have formed key social units within Copán with water-management devolved to elites within these groups, who may have taken primary responsibility for the offerings and feasts attested by archaeological remains within and around these lagoons (Davis-Salazar 2003).

Davis-Salazar (2006) notes that drainage and flood control installations exhibit very different construction techniques and materials, both between different residential clusters and between such clusters and the principal architectural group at Copán. She credits this difference to the various water-hole groups being responsible for the construction and management of drainage systems in their own neighbourhood. The rulers of Copán are said to have coordinated water management at a valley-wide level, perhaps by overseeing interaction between these various water-hole groups by means of a council (Fash and Davis Salazar 2006). Rulers also took central place in the ritual cycle viewed as essential for renewing and controlling water supplies.

In both Copán and Tikal, water management and water ritual have been linked to each other and to a central political authority, but in distinct ways and with reference to distinct mechanisms. One could also consider the case of Palenque, another large regional centre located in a water-rich area in Chiapas (the site's Maya name, *Lakamha'*, means 'wide waters'; see French et al. 2006: 145). The site has 41 known water sources within its boundary, as well as nine watercourses that flow through it (French 2007; French et al. 2006). It also possesses a rich collection of iconography related to water-ritual, especially in the ritual connection made between sweat-baths and caves at the site (Child 2007). Like Copán, water management at Palenque is oriented towards flood control, although the system at Palenque seems to be more uniform across the site and, therefore, perhaps centrally planned (Davis-Salazar 2006). However, water-management at Palenque does not create resources to draw farmers in from outlying areas (where, after all, water would be available all year round). Rather, at Palenque, water-management helped to create the site itself, in that the main plaza is raised above drainage conduits that canalise the flood-prone watercourses, and extended over uneven ground that would not otherwise support large-scale architecture (French 2007). In other words, large-scale water-management is linked to political power, not because it ensures that centralisation is the only option, but because it creates the possibility of living in a particular way. Without centralised water-management there would still be dispersed Maya farmers, but there would be no Tikal, Copán or Palenque.

Lucero (2006) argues that riverine centres differ from those in the lowland karst zone in that settlement density is higher in the immediate vicinity of sites such as Copán or Palenque. According to Lucero, this limits the mobility of farmers and allows rulers to control access to land as well as to water. By making riverine centres a special case, however, Lucero overlooks the clear symmetry between highland and lowland regional centres. She does this in the interest of preserving a causative link between her settlement types and the centralised control of still-water reserves in the lowlands. But is this link worth preserving? Making the control of still-water reserves determinative inevitably leads us into 'chicken or egg' arguments regarding the origins of water dependency vis-à-vis social inequality; it also reduces ritual to a kind of false consciousness and it draws our attention away from the common 'world building' practices of Maya rulers in both water-rich and water-poor regions.

It would be more productive to reframe the relationship between water management and water ritual in Mayan kingdoms in terms of our discussions of hegemony and the techniques of sovereignty. There is no doubt that water was a central resource (both materially and culturally) for the Maya, and that rulership amongst the Maya was constituted through practices that included the physical and ritual management of water (amongst other key resources such as maize, ancestors and blood). Supplying water and ensuring its renewal via essential rituals was a kind of public good, one that articulated widely shared Mayan ideas and practices regarding how the cosmos was ordered and how one survived and prospered in this world. It provided, therefore, one basis for consent to sovereignty in Gramsci's terms (see Chapter 2).

At the same time, centralised rule was not the only, or even the best, way to live in this region. Indeed, resource distribution, especially in the lowlands, favours dispersed settlement. Hence, the physical and ritual management of water was a public good relative to particular interests and in the perceived absence of certain options (like seasonal mobility). The hegemony of Mayan kings required the constant assertion that 'the way things are, is the way things are'. This involved strategic practices asserting the centrality of kingship to the reproduction of the social and cosmological order, practices that raised the cost of non-compliance, and practices that caused kingship to fade into the background as the setting for everyday life through the built environment, the seasonality of ritual observance, and the provision of stored water.

Such techniques of sovereignty cannot be partitioned into the spectacular and the routine, as each involves the possibility of both active reflection and embodied habituation. Drawing water ingeniously collected from the run-off of a temple platform and standing in a crowd to watch rulers impersonate the water-lily serpent contain elements of both the spectacular and the routine. These elements not only co-exist, they also co-determine one another. Water management, in both the physical and cosmological sense, routinised the spectacle of grand architecture and ritual observance by ordering lives to be lived in a particular way. These were lives in which one drank water from this reservoir, irrigated one's fields from that channel, and ensured the renewal of rainfall by making these offerings in that temple, or by participating in this dance in that plaza. In other words, the basic 'scaffolding' of life in a Mayan centre constituted the centrality of Mayan rulers, even as that centrality provided a meaningful explanation for the order and continued existence of this particular way of life. That this was not the only life that Mayans could imagine or live is evident in the difficulties Mayan rulers experienced in attracting and retaining subjects.

Summation

In this chapter, I have argued that the practices, strategies and relationships that constitute a given political order involve elements of both symbolic representation and habit memory; they are simultaneously spectacular and routine. It remains for us to consider how this all fits together, how sovereignty emerges from spectacular and routine practices that draw together and create interdependent elements within a given historical bloc under a specific logic of hegemony. Of particular concern is something we have yet to address directly, the violence at the heart of sovereignty, those relations of force that set limits on what interests hegemony will articulate. It is not insignificant, for example, that besides the life-giving substances of water and maize, the other substance central to Mayan kingship was blood. How can the spectacle of violence, which inherently pits the interests of some against others, be routinised and subsumed within the social performances of hegemony? In the next chapter we will take up this question through an extended case study of the Royal Tombs of Ur.

6

Routine lives and spectacular deaths

The Royal Tombs of Ur

Hoe, do not start getting so mightily angry! Do not be so mightily
scornful! Is not Nisaba *the Hoe's inspector? Is not* Nisaba *its overseer?*
The scribe will register your work, he will register your work. Hoe,
whether he enters five or 10 giĝ in your account, Hoe – or, Hoe,
whether he enters one-third or one-half mana in your account, Hoe,
like a maid-servant, always ready, you will fulfil your task.

'The Debate between Hoe and Plough'
(ETCSL translation t.5.3.1: lines 186–93)

Between 1926 and 1934 Leonard Woolley excavated and documented
some 2,110 tombs dating to the third millennium BC and positioned
adjacent to the temple of Nanna the moon god at the site of Ur
(modern Tall al-Muqayyar) in southern Iraq (see Woolley 1934; 1955;
Figures 6.1 and 6.2). Sixteen of these tombs, all belonging to the Early
Dynastic IIIA period (ca. 2600–2450 BC), were designated as 'Royal
Tombs' by Woolley due to: 1) their constructed tomb chambers;
2) the abundance and wealth of their grave goods; and 3) the elaborate
nature of their interment rituals, including evidence for the ritual
killing or mass suicide of numerous attendants (Woolley 1934: 33–42).
Eighty years on, the 'Royal Tombs of Ur' remain one the world's
most spectacular archaeological discoveries (e.g. Zettler and Horne
1998). In part, this is a product of the exquisitely crafted objects in
rare materials that the tombs contained and the archetypal narrative
of Woolley's patient endeavour in excavating and conserving these
objects. However, our continued fascination with the Royal Tombs is

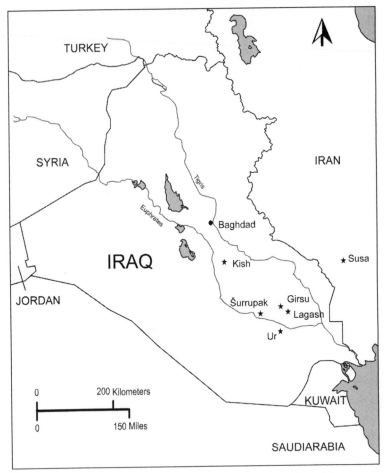

Figure 6.1   Map of Mesopotamia showing sites mentioned in text

also due to the incongruity, indeed the mystery, of intentional killings regularised in large-scale funerary ceremonies. In what follows I will use the Royal Tombs of Ur to explore how the routinised violence of sovereignty is revealed in the exceptional violence of funerary spectacles in Early Dynastic Ur.

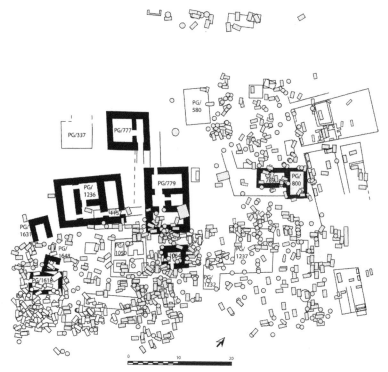

Figure 6.2   General plan of the 'Royal Cemetery of Ur' (redrawn from Woolley 1934, Plate 274)

Tombs, attendants and mortuary spectacles

Woolley (1934: 33–8) argued that all 16 of the Royal Tombs of Ur shared a common burial pattern. Each tomb contained a deep vertical shaft, with an access ramp on one side, at the bottom of which was constructed in stone or brick either: a) a single-chambered tomb with an open forecourt in front; or b) a multi-chambered tomb consisting of a primary and one or more secondary chambers. In 13 of the tombs the excavators noted the presence of more than one individual; in the other three (PG/580, PG/1236 and PG/1631) human bones were too poorly preserved or highly disturbed to identify individuals. In many cases the number of bodies interred together was very high, with the six most populous tombs containing between 22 (PG/800) and 74 (PG/1237) bodies. In many cases it was also possible to identify a principal burial, due to its location in the primary tomb chamber, its burial in a coffin or on a podium, and the wealth of its associated grave goods. Most famous in this regard is Queen Pu-abi, so identified by an inscribed cylinder seal. Most of the bodies in these tombs, however, were located in secondary chambers or in the open forecourts in front of the single chamber tombs. Woolley (1934: 33) dubbed these forecourts 'death pits', suggesting that the bodies therein were attendants killed for the express purpose of inclusion in their master's or mistress's tomb.

Many scholars, including Woolley (1934: 41) himself, have noted that the highly structured nature of the Royal Tomb deposits appears to be the outcome of elaborate ritual acts (e.g. Baadsgaard et al. 2012; Cohen 2005; Vidale 2011; Winter 2009). Bodies were both carefully laid out and carefully dressed, at times with jewellery, personal items or functionally specific tools, weapons and instruments executed in valuable raw materials with a very high level of craftsmanship. There also appear to be clear groupings and associations of bodies. Most obvious are the groups of armed 'soldiers' near several of the entrances, the bodies of 'grooms' found beneath the skeletons of oxen teams still harnessed to carts or sledges, and those of 'musicians' found adjacent to Ur's famous lyres and harp. The limited number of skeletal remains examined by Molleson and Hogson (1993; 2000; 2003: 125–7) suggested task-specific muscular development and osteopathologies for certain individuals, as well as a relative absence of such features on the principal occupants of tombs, including for example Queen Pu-abi. While uncertainty regarding the criteria for curation make the Ur skeletons a problematic sample, these results do support the commonsense inference that in life individuals buried in the Royal Tombs occupied the same roles (e.g. 'porter', 'cart/sledge driver', elite) in which they had been cast in death.

Beyond these well-known examples, there also appear to be systematic patterns in the distribution of jewellery, especially headdresses, within the tombs (see Gansell 2007). For example, whereas most of the crania

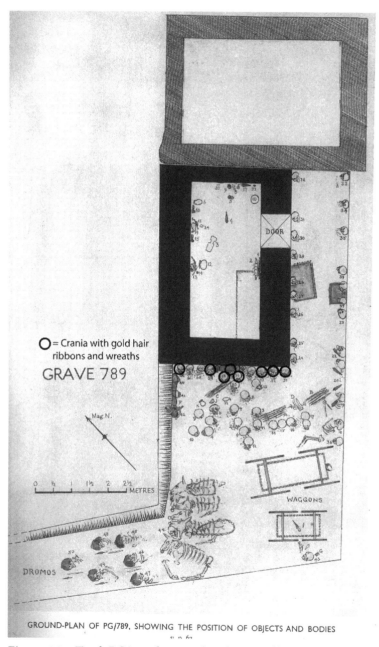

GROUND-PLAN OF PG/789, SHOWING THE POSITION OF OBJECTS AND BODIES

Figure 6.3   Tomb PG/789 showing distribution of hair adornment on bodies (after Woolley 1934, Plate 29)

in tomb PG/789 (Figure 6.3) were associated with either silver hair rings or no headdresses, at least eight of the eleven bodies laid out in a row against the outside of the south-western wall of the tomb chamber were associated with gold hair ribbons and wreaths and only one was associated with silver rings (Woolley 1934: 65–7, Pl. 29). Similarly, while the majority of the bodies in the centre of the 'Great Death Pit' (PG/1237) were dressed with gold hair ribbons and wreaths, none of the bodies in the outermost rows (along the north-east and south-west

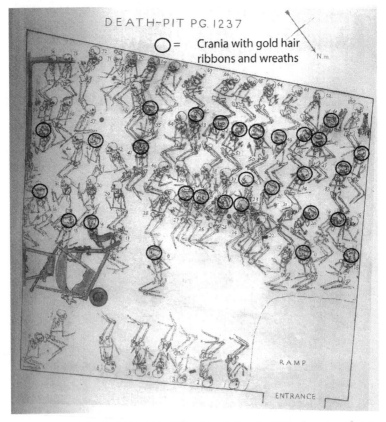

Figure 6.4   Tomb PG/1237 ('The Great Death Pit') showing distribution of hair adornment on bodies (after Woolley 1934, Plate 71)

walls of the pit) were dressed in this manner, most being adorned with gold earrings and chokers (Figure 6.4).

Overall, the jewellery suggests that the attendants were adorned and positioned within the tomb groups in a highly structured manner that may reflect their roles in life or in the funerary ritual (see also Vidale 2011). Alternatively, these patterns could reflect an overall aesthetic for the burial events planned around the structured alteration of adorned bodies (e.g. placing attendants in rows in terms of contrasting jewellery).

Woolley suggested that the regular arrangement of the bodies and their active association with musical instruments, weapons or teams of oxen indicated that these attendants had died where they lay without violent struggle after participating in an elaborate funerary procession. This, and the common association of cups with bodies in the Royal Cemetery, led Woolley to posit that the attendants in the Royal Tombs had voluntarily committed suicide by drinking some form of poison or sedative (Woolley 1934: 35–6). In Woolley's words the 'death pits' represented a royal court '… going with their master to continue to serve under new conditions, possibly even assuring themselves thereby of a less nebulous and miserable existence in the afterworld than was the lot of men dying in the ordinary way' (Woolley 1934: 42).

That the attendants went peacefully to their deaths, as Woolley believed, is, however, open to question. Recent analysis of CT-scans of the crania of one male soldier (body 50 in PG/789) and one female attendant (body 52 in PG/1237) in the University of Pennsylvania Museum's collection, suggests that both were killed by blunt force trauma, probably with a narrow-bladed axe (Baadsgaard et al. 2011: 32–7). Evidence also suggests that the female may have been heated and treated with cinnabar (mercuric sulphide) as a preservation measure (Baadsgaard et al. 2011: 37–8).

Woolley (1934: 142) had already noted that many of the bodies in the Ur cemetery appeared to have been 'lightly burned', and a reanalysis of the curated skeletons in the Natural History Museum (London) confirmed a prolonged heating of the bodies, much as in the case of the University of Pennsylvania Museum sample (Molleson and Hogson 2003: 123). Hence, it seems likely that the regular arrangements of the bodies in the best preserved 'death pits' (e.g. PG/789, PG/800, PG/1237) were the outcome of the post-mortem preservation and manipulation of the attendants' bodies, rather than peaceful, *in situ*, deaths (cf. Baadsgaard et al. 2011: 39–40). In light of all of this evidence, the Royal Tombs appear to be a kind of macabre *tableau*, planned around the primary interment and realised with the bodies of attendants killed and preserved specifically for this purpose (Vidale 2011).

Clearly, in the case of the Royal Tombs of Ur, we are dealing with large-scale spectacles that even in the present day retain their ability to both fascinate and disturb. In the words of Roger Moorey (1977: 40) this was 'clearly a special rite for special people'. Yet, admitting the uniquely spectacular nature of these burial practices simply underlines the problem of how and why such rites occurred. The attendants' deaths were not random acts of violence but highly ordered and regularised events. What practices and relationships made these deaths possible? How were these attendants constituted as 'killable subjects' (Agamben 1998), either in their own minds or in the minds of others (*cf.* Pollock 2007a: 89–90)?

Some scholars have looked to formal rituals attested in Mesopotamian texts in order to explain the striking burial practices of the Royal Tombs. Early on, it was suggested that the tombs might contain substitute kings, whose ritual killing to save the sitting king from bad omens is sporadically attested in the second and first millennia BC (Frankfort 1948: 264, 400n. 12). More commonly, scholars have wondered if the tombs might represent the interments of the principal figures of sacred marriage rituals tied to the New Year festival, whether directly as part of the ritual (e.g. Moortgat 1949) or at the end of their lives as a reflection of the elevated status such a role bestowed upon them (Moorey 1977: 40).

Other scholars have connected the funerary rites of the Royal Tombs with descriptions of death and the netherworld in Sumerian literature (e.g. Tinney 1998). In the fragmentary *Death of Gilgamesh*, for example, it appears that the hero king Gilgamesh is buried with:

> ... [h]is beloved wife, his beloved children, his beloved favourite and junior wife, his beloved musician, cup-bearer and ... his beloved barber, his beloved ... his beloved palace retainers and servants and his beloved objects ...' (ETCSL translation t.1.8.1.3: Nibru fragment lines 1–7)

On the very next line of the same tablet Gilgamesh presents valuable gifts to Ereškigala, lady of the underworld, as well as to numerous deities and dead notables. Presumably this allows Gilgamesh to assume the role of ruler in the underworld, as was foretold to him on his deathbed. In *The Death of Ur-Namma* (ETCSL t.2.4.1.1), the king Ur-Namma is said to be buried with his donkeys and to present gifts and host an opulent banquet for the important figures of the underworld on his arrival in order to secure a worthy position.

More sociologically minded scholars explain the exceptional nature of the Royal Tombs by arguing that they occur at a moment of historical crisis in the transition from charismatic to hereditary (or religious to secular) rule. Andrew Cohen (2005: 147–54) has argued that the exceptional display of the Royal Tombs is a by-product of the emergence of new forms of kingship based on lineage and inherited authority, albeit still embedded in temple ritual. In this early stage the transition between rulers following the king's death was an unstable and uncertain time that needed to be negotiated by means of elaborate funerary rituals emphasising the power, legitimacy and continuity of the ruling lineage (*cf.* Redman 1978: 297–8). While accepting a similar historical context, Bruce Dickson (2006) posits the more blunt function of intimidation and terror for these funerary rituals, calling them 'public transcripts of cruelty' aimed at frightening subjects into continued submission. In contrast, Susan Pollock (2007a; 2007b) argues that the Royal Tombs represent the last gasp of institutional households based on principles of charismatic leadership (such as divine selection), with their conspicuous destruction of wealth and labour making an extreme statement against the inherited forms of power emerging during the Early Dynastic period.

Two sorts of problems plague both those who appeal to culturally specific ritual and those who appeal to a general social transition. The first is empirical. In the case of formal rituals, as Woolley (1934: 37–42) himself already argued in his publication of the Ur Cemetery, the links drawn to textual sources are very weak. References to the killing of substitute kings in Assyria occur more than a millennium after the Royal Tombs, are ambiguous, and do not entail large entourages of attendants. Similarly, the sacred marriage rite, where the king assumes the role of the god Dumuzi and a priestess the role of the goddess Inanna in order to ensure the annual renewal of agricultural fertility, did not entail ritual killing, focuses on a sacred couple rather than single principal burials as found in the Royal Tombs and, according to some recent scholarship, may have existed only as a literary image rather than as an actual ritual (see Lapinkivi 2004 for literature).

Unfortunately, although *The Death of Gilgamesh* may provide a literary attestation of attendant burials as seen in the Royal Tombs (but see Marchesi 2004: 156–60), it provides no real insight into why such practices occurred. Gift giving and banqueting on the entry into the underworld in *The Death of Gilgamesh* and most especially in *The Death of Ur-Namma* may provide an internal rationale for the wealth of the grave goods found in the Royal Tombs, as well as the clear link between the tombs and contemporary banqueting scenes (see pp. 141–8). However, one is still left to wonder how and why this could justify the mass killings attested in the Royal Tombs.

In terms of explaining the Royal Tombs as an ideological response to a social transition, we should remember that the presumed trajectory from 'charismatic' religious leadership to inherited and institution-alised secular/military leadership in Mesopotamia is largely a scholarly reconstruction. Some scholars posit an internal evolution spurred on by the necessities of military conflict and aggressive expansion (e.g. Frankfort 1948: 215–26; Jacobsen 1957). Others posit a growing dominance of northern Mesopotamian traditions of inherited kingship over southern Mesopotamian traditions of temple-based leadership and divinely-sanctioned selection (Heimpel 1992). While either of these may have happened, currently available evidence does not allow us to presume that either trend did happen (Zettler 1998: 29). As is well known, the first phases of urbanised social life in Mesopotamia, namely the Late Uruk (ca. 3400–3100 BC) and Jemdat Nasr (ca. 3100–2800 BC) periods, already attest most of the material trappings of centralised rule. Besides cities, large temple precincts and our earliest written texts, the city of Uruk also attests standardised images of the so-called 'priest-king' in a variety of media (Vogel 2008: 83–134). This figure, wearing a net skirt and a headdress oddly reminiscent of a bowler hat, is depicted in a variety of key kingly activities that are both religious and martial in character. It is true that the word for palace, *é-gal* (lit. 'big house'), first appears in the Early Dynastic IIIA period (ca. 2600–2450 BC), roughly contemporary with the Royal Tombs, but the import of this fact is unclear, especially given the limited and ambiguous nature of the archaic texts found prior to ED IIIA.

In the ED IIIA–B periods, the three primary titles for city leaders in Sumerian, *en*, *ensik* and *lugal*, are used simultaneously and at times interchangeably, by the rulers of distinct Sumerian city-states (see examples in Cooper 1986). More to the point, even if the earliest Sumerian city-states were ruled by someone called an *en* and this office was displaced in the Early Dynastic period by the offices of *ensik* and *lugal*, we have no direct evidence for how individuals were appointed to the office of *en*. Early Dynastic royal inscriptions show that both *ensik* and *lugal* could be inherited, or at least held by father, son and grandson. The *en*, in contrast, may have been an appointed, charismatic leader legitimised by his religious role (e.g. Heimpel 1992), but in truth we do not know. In fact, our best evidence for claims of divine selection, of being selected 'from among the myriad of people', to use Cooper's translation (1986: La 5.18; La 9.1), come not from Uruk or from priestly contexts, but from the standard titular of the Early Dynastic IIIB (ca. 2450–2350 BC) rulers of Lagash. Most of these rulers can be shown to be the direct descendants of previous rulers of Lagash and all of them claim the title *ensik* or *lugal*, or both. In other words, in the fragmentary evidence available to us the only rulers claiming to be chosen by the gods are those who seem to have inherited the title from their fathers. The supposed evolution from charismatic to inherited authority cannot be demonstrated directly, but must be presumed to exist in the many gaps conveniently present in the available evidence.

This said, even if we cannot presume a religious/charismatic to secular/institutional transition, it remains the case that the Early Dynastic Period, and especially ED III, is a period of significant social and political change. For example, regional surveys indicate that both the size of urban centres and the proportion of the population living in such centres in southern Mesopotamia peaked during the ED III period (Pollock 1999: 45–77). Hence cities, and presumably also their temple institutions and military and political leaders, were playing a larger role in the lives of more people than ever before. Furthermore, ED IIIB inscriptions make clear that the rulers of these urban centres were competing fiercely to control land, people and each other; attempting to forge new, larger-scale political units via conquest and patronage. In other words, one can make a rather strong case that the Royal Tombs were built at a time when political institutions and community identities were in flux.

So, one might still explain the exceptional nature of the Royal Tombs in terms of some sort of legitimation crisis on the basis of broader evidence for social change in the ED III period. However, the exceptional nature of the burial rites attested in the Royal Tombs presents a second, more significant problem if one is seeking to situate these rites within some sort of general explanation (be it formal ritual or social crisis). If the Royal Tombs are the outcome of some general social or political transition in Southern Mesopotamia, then why do we not find other Royal Tombs in, say Uruk, or Umma or Lagash? Certainly, sampling and survival play a major role, but as several scholars have stressed (Moorey 1977; Selz 2004), even within Ur these burial rites constitute an exceptional case.

Elaborate and wealthy third-millennium tombs have been found elsewhere in Mesopotamia (e.g. Eickhoff 1993; Pollock 1999: 205–17). Indeed, tombs containing carts and oxen/donkey teams are known (if poorly documented) from Susa in south-western Iran (Mecquenem 1943: 103–4, 122–3) and Kish in northern Babylon (Moorey 1978: 104–10). The three (semi-) published chariot tombs from Kish have been compared to the Royal Tombs at Ur, as they may have been constructed as a deep shaft with a ramp (Moorey 1978: 104–6) and there are multiple bodies in several of the tombs. However, to quote Seton Lloyd (1969: 48), the Kish tombs were 'badly excavated, the excavations were badly recorded and the records were correspondingly badly published' (Lloyd 1969: 48). As a result, it is very difficult to reconstruct burial practices in these tombs, and indeed, after examining the unpublished field records, Guillermo Algaze denied any parallels with Ur beyond the presence of animal-drawn carts (see Algaze 1983/4: 149–54). Where scholars do agree is that, in terms of material wealth and overall organisation, the chariot burials at Kish are not at all comparable to the Royal Tombs of Ur (Moorey 1978: 105–6; Algaze 1983/4: 153–4).

Moorey resolves the problem posed by the exceptional nature of the Royal Tombs by stating that the key may lie 'with a cult practice special to Ur', since '[t]he Sumerian city-states each had their own peculiar traditions and we are still far from understanding many of them in their own terms' (Moorey 1977: 39). Moorey is correct in the narrow sense that these burial customs are specific to Ur and their proximate causes may never be known given the available evidence. At the same time, Moorey's solution is inadequate in the larger sense of understanding how and why the conspicuous consumption and ritual killings attested to in these tombs came to be seen as a suitable expression of whatever local circumstances may have prevailed in Early Dynastic Ur.

Despite their exceptional nature, the Royal Tombs are clearly structured by, and embedded in, symbols, values, materials and ideas that were widely distributed in Early Dynastic Sumer. We must, therefore,

Figure 6.5 'Peace' side of the Royal Standard of Ur showing a banquet scene (source: ©The Trustees of the British Museum)

ask how the exceptional spectacle of ritual killings and conspicuous consumption found in the Royal Tombs might have arisen from, and found acceptance within, the more routine workings of Sumerian society in the mid-third millennium BC In other words, we need to look at how this exception might prove the rule of rule in Early Dynastic Sumer.

One rather striking feature of the Royal Tombs is the way in which they reference elite banqueting practices in multiple ways. Banquet scenes are a generic theme in Early Dynastic art (Schmandt-Besserat 2001). Typically, the core of each scene is a pair of seated figures drinking from cups or from a common pot via straws and being attended to by servants. Banquet scenes are amongst the most common themes on cylinder seals from the Royal Cemetery of Ur, including the seal of Pu-abi herself. Beyond this, one finds banquet scenes elsewhere in the Royal Tombs as inlaid decoration on the sound boxes of lyres (Woolley 1934: Pl. 116) and most famously on the 'Standard of Ur' (Woolley 1934: 266–74). Here the so-called 'Peace' side of the Standard includes a banquet scene, with a procession of servants bringing bounty to a larger-than-life-size figure drinking with his guests in the upper register (Figure 6.5).

Many scholars (Baadsgaard et al., 2012; Cohen 2005; Pollock 2003; 2007a; Selz 2004) have commented on the ways in which the bodies and grave goods in the Royal Tombs have been laid out to suggest participation in a banquet. Andrew Cohen (2005: 82–93, 167–220), for example, has shown that the ceramic assemblages in the Royal Tombs are largely limited to serving and eating vessels, with a notable paucity of cooking and long-term storage vessels. Woolley (1934: 36) himself commented on the frequency of drinking vessels in the Royal Tombs, with many being proximate to the hands of individual skeletons. Interestingly, one also finds many distinct artefacts in the Royal Tombs that are themselves depicted in banquet scenes.

One rather notable example is the occurrence of bull-headed and bull-shaped lyres in the Royal Tombs (Woolley 1934: 249–58, Pls 107–21), along with depictions of such lyres in banquet scenes on

Figure 6.6 Soundbox of lyre (U. 10556) from tomb PG/789 showing a satirical banquet scene with animals and mythological creatures (source: University of Pennsylvania Museum, Image Number 150888, Object Number B17694)

cylinder seals (Woolley 1934: 21–2, Pl. 193,), on the 'Standard of Ur' (Woolley 1934: 266–74, Pl. 91) and on the sound box of one of the lyres itself (Woolley 1934: Pl. 105; see Figure 6.6). Bull-shaped lyres are also depicted at other mid-third millennium sites on cylinder seals (Amiet 1980: Pl.91:1200–1201) and stone plaques (Boese 1971: Taf.17: 1), showing that this very particular object was intimately linked to the representation of elite banqueting practices across Early Dynastic Sumer. Through such dense, and very specific, cross-referencing we see how deeply embedded the Royal Tombs were in the themes, imagery and material culture of elite life in mid-third millennium Sumer. Indeed, one could go so far as to say that the carefully placed bodies and objects of the Royal Tombs were simply another medium for the representation of banquet scenes.

Banqueting in early Mesopotamia was linked to two key moral requirements, namely feeding the gods and feeding the dead (Jagersma 2007). These obligations included regular food and libation offerings, as well as large-scale festivals and feasts. Interestingly, libation scenes on cylinder seals (Amiet 1980: Pl. 100–3) and stone plaques (Boese 1971: Taf. 18: 1–4; 21: 4) bear some parallels to banquet scenes, with priests and other elite mortals acting in the role of servants pouring out liquids before seated deities holding cups. Irene Winter (2009) has pointed to sets of pouring vessels in many of the Ur tombs that match those of libations scenes. While Winter's emphasis on the multiple uses of such pouring vessels is suitably cautious, it remains likely that these burial rites involved libations like those performed for deities.

With their analogical connection to the provisioning of the gods and their direct connection to the provisioning of the dead, funerary feasts would seem to be doubly marked as significant events in the ritual life of Mesopotamia. Yet, neither this symbolic content, nor the various social and political functions ascribed to feasting and commensal politics in the comparative literature, seems to satisfactorily explain the exceptional nature of the Royal Tombs.

Brian Hayden, for example, has argued that elaborate funerary feasts are cross-culturally significant in what he terms trans-egalitarian and early state societies (Hayden 2009). For Hayden this significance stems from the fact that, in directing attention to the dead, funerals are lifecycle rituals that allow morally acceptable ostentation. As such, they provide a context for expanding and reinforcing alliances through the gifting of food, as well as a context for signalling group wealth and success (Hayden 2001; 2009). In particular, Hayden's 'political ecology' asks that we look past the specific symbolic content of the Royal Tombs, and focus on the supposed adaptive function of elaborate funerary feasts as a stage for forming and affirming alliances and clientship.

In keeping with Hayden's cross-cultural model, elite funerals in Early Dynastic Mesopotamia do seem to have involved large disbursements of food and drink to lower-ranking individuals. Two ED IIIB (2450–2350 BC) texts from Girsu show that the reigning queen Šagšag twice dispersed large amounts of bread and beer to lamentation specialists (*gala*), 'wives of elders', male relatives of the deceased and female temple servants (a total of 618 people) involved in mourning rites for Bara-namtara, her predecessor as queen (Cohen 2005: 56–7, 157–62; Jagersma 2007: 293–4; Selz 2004: 198–9). Admittedly, it is not clear that these disbursements were viewed as acts of hospitality or as payment for service as mourners. For example, in his famous reforms, Šagšag's husband Uru-inimgina, king of Lagash, seems to stipulate a set fee in bread and beer to be given to lamentation specialists and 'old women' during rites of mourning (Cooper 1986: La 9.2). At the same time, the wider corpus of ED IIIB texts from Girsu indicates that large numbers of people attached to an institution headed by the Queen of Lagash, known as the 'house of the woman' (*é-mí*) and later the 'house of the goddess Bau' (*é-ᵈba-ú*), shared in disbursements of food and drink from the institution's stores during religious festivals throughout the year (Beld 2002: 96–196; Jagersma 2007: 303–8). So, the fact of large feasts, in which elites provided food and drink to their clients, dependants and subordinates, is well established for Early Dynastic Mesopotamia.

This said, looking beyond the specific symbolic content of the Royal Tombs to its adaptive function is not as simple as Hayden implies. While the burial events surrounding the Royal Tombs may have involved feasting, the tombs themselves are also *representations* of feasts; in other words it is their symbolic content that tells us these are feasts in the first place. Furthermore, if the real story of funerary feasts is always and only one of building advantageous alliances, one might wonder if killing attendants was really an effective recruitment strategy! There is no doubt that clientship and other forms of dependency were a vitally important component of banqueting in Early Dynastic Mesopotamia (see Beld 2002). However, as we shall see in a moment, it is impossible to analyse such relations without reference to the institutional framework (especially temple and palace households) and specific economic relationships within which this dependency was realised.

Somewhat better suited to discussing the Royal Tombs as representations of feasts might be Michael Dietler's category of the 'diacritical feast' (Dietler 2001). For Dietler, feasts in hierarchical societies sometimes cease to be vehicles for forming and reinforcing dyadic relations and social solidarity. Rather, they can serve to emphasize social distinctions and provide a venue for intra-class social competition. For Dietler, diacritical feasts are marked by the emphasis on signs of exclusivity: exotic foods, highly marked and often expensive accoutrements and settings; as well as elaborate preparations and practices that imply specialised knowledge. While we have only limited knowledge regarding the foods included in the Royal Tombs (see Ellison et al. 1978), the gold, silver, lapis lazuli and ostrich eggshell vessels (Woolley 1934: Pls 156–7, 160–5, 170–4), the gold, silver, copper and lapis lazuli drinking straws (Weber and Zettler 1998: 139), the ivory, turquoise and shell inlaid musical instruments and furniture (Woolley 1934: Pls 91–126), the elaborate jewellery (Woolley 1934: Pls 127–50) and virtually everything else found in the Royal Tombs fit well with Dietler's definition of a diacritical feast.

While Early Dynastic banquets were certainly represented as marked events of an elite nature, it is less clear that they were represented in terms of competitive gifting – what Marcel Mauss (1990: 6–7) termed agonistic exchange. Denise Schmandt-Besserat (2001) points to the Sumerian literary composition 'The Debate between Winter and Summer' (ETCSL t.5.3.3) as an example of such elite competition. A close examination of this text, however, reveals something rather interesting about feasting and social competition in Sumer. There are two incidents in the story that might be classified as feasts. Initially, as part of competing to be acknowledged as the superior season, Winter and Summer contend by attempting to outdo each other in their presentation of food offerings to the god Enlil in his temple. However, once Enlil declares that Winter is superior (because Winter's water makes Summer's harvest possible), Summer hosts Winter in his home and presents him with beer, wine, a banquet of succulent food, as well as gifts of gold, silver and lapis lazuli; pouring out 'brotherhood and friendship like oil' and 'bringing sweet words to the quarrel' (ETCSL translation t.5.3.3: lines 310–15). In other words, the context in which Winter and Summer are competing is not as hosts, but as fellow worshippers (and hence servants) currying the favour of Enlil in his own house (i.e. his temple). This competition is not left open; rather, a hierarchical order is established through Enlil's declaration of Winter's superiority. Summer hosts Winter in his home in order to end their competition, re-establish their relationship and acknowledge Winter's superior rank.

While social competition is likely to have played a role in the actual dynamics of Early Dynastic banqueting, it is not the prime emphasis of the visual and literary representations of banqueting in which the Royal Tombs participates. Rather than competitive exchange between elites, representations of feasts in Early Dynastic Sumer would seem to celebrate, and incorporate guests into, already established hierarchies marked by the upward movement of abundance. Most obvious is the presentation of offerings to deities who were the principal guests at religious festivals held in their honour. However, there is also an emphasis on the provisioning of the central celebrants whose drinking from cups or straws stands at the centre of most banquet scenes.

A striking aspect of Early Dynastic banqueting scenes is their stress on service. In most cases, servants equal or outnumber banqueters in these scenes, and, in the more elaborate scenes with multiple registers, the portage and presentation of consumables takes up the bulk of the visual field. In the case of the banquet scene on the 'Standard of Ur', there is a literal upward movement of service as those in the lower two registers seem to be processing animals and goods towards the large central figure and his banqueting companions in the upper register, as if the entire scene culminated in their acts of consumption (see Figure 6.5).

The thematic importance of service and servants is also highlighted by examples of satirical banqueting scenes in which animals take the role of humans (see Amiet 1980: Pl. 99). On the soundbox (U. 10556) of one of the lyres from the Royal Tombs (Woolley 1934: Pl. 105) we have a three register scene, in which animals and mythical creatures appear as musicians and servants in a banquet context and the upper register is occupied by a 'hero' figure in the 'master of the animals' pose between two recumbent 'bull-men' (Figure 6.6). Less subtle is an Early Dynastic IIIA cylinder seal from Ur (Figure 6.7), predating the Royal Cemetery, on which an ibex, three equids and several small mammals provide music, drink and food for a seated lion (Legrain 1936: Pl. 20:384). As if to make sure that the message is not missed, to the right of the satirical banquet scene is an animal combat scene in which a lioness is using a dagger to attack an ungulate. Anthropomorphised in this way, servants become the prey and sustenance of those whom they serve. At the same time, the very fact that this relationship of service is satirised highlights its centrality to the genre of banquet scenes. In other words, servants in the act of service may be secondary and subordinate *within* Sumerian banquet scenes, but they are primary *to* those scenes in the sense of conveying their central message.

In one sense, in emphasizing service in Sumerian banquet scenes I am simply pointing to the second of Dietler's two characteristics of diacritical feasting; stressing the reproduction of class divisions rather than intra-class competition between elite banqueters. However, we should remember that priests and rulers take this same role of servant when providing food offerings or libations for deities. Indeed, to quote

Figure 6.7 Early Dynastic seal from Ur featuring a satirical banquet scene with animals (source: LeGrain 1936: Plate 20 no. 384)

Igor Diakonoff, from a representational point of view, in the third millennium BC 'no person is without his or her lord (human or divine), and thus … everyone is someone's slave' (Diakonoff 1987: 2). In other words, in Early Dynastic Sumer the theme of service was subsumed into a larger representational order that emphasized upwardly oriented relations of obligation. In this sense, the representation of service in banquet scenes did not merely aim to reproduce those immediate class divisions. Instead, banquet scenes encompassed service in a world defined by obligations to superiors, including obligations to the gods, and thereby sought to rationalise everyday class divisions in terms that were ultimately cosmological.

Susan Pollock (2007a; 2007b) has long stressed that the key link between all of the Early Dynastic burials in the Ur cemetery, and most particularly the Royal Tombs, was membership in the large institutional households that structured the political economy of Early Dynastic Sumer. Certainly, as Gianni Marchesi (2004: 175–81) has shown, epigraphic evidence from the Royal Tombs provides strong support for the assertion that at least some of the principal female burials bore the title 'nin', meaning 'lady' and designating high status (Marchesi 2004: 186–9). This suggests that we are on safe ground in connecting the Royal Tombs to at least one of the major institutional households of Ur. Which one seems less significant if members of the same families were controlling both temple and palace households in given cites or polities, as is suggested by Girsu texts. In other words, while Early Dynastic Sumerian polities were not temple-states, it seems likely that the palace and major temples did form a core that constituted what might be called a governmental apparatus and an inner elite, to which the principal burials in the Royal Tombs seem to have belonged.

For Pollock (2007a: 100; 2007b: 216–17) the Royal Tombs represent the symbolic death of one these great households upon the death of one its principal figures. She suggests that middle- and upper-ranking members of an institutional household, along with the household's symbolically valuable possessions, would have joined the principal deceased figure in death through participation in an actual or symbolic funerary banquet in the tomb itself (Pollock 2007a: 102n. 8; 2007b: 214). As noted above, Pollock (2007b: 216–18) believes that this display of extreme loyalty to a household was a dramatic public expression of traditional, divinely determined and uninheritable leadership, against a rising tide of inherited, dynastic power. Pollock (2007a: 100–6) suggests that the willingness of these courtiers to go to their own death was an outcome of their constitution as 'docile bodies' in the regular workings of large institutional households. Most particularly, Pollock (2007a: 101–5) argues that routine participation in formal banquets, performing specific roles with specific expectations, would help inculcate one's relative rank and obligations as embodied practice (i.e. habit-memory). Pollock suggests that this routinisation of one's identification within the institutional household would make following one's lord or lady into the tomb less a matter of choice than of expectation.

Essentially, Pollock is arguing that the Royal Tombs were constituted by both spectacle and routine; that the extreme logic of the funerary spectacle was embedded in the routine logic of regular banqueting practices. At the broadest level this explanation is compelling. If the ritual killings of the Royal Tombs were understood as the logical outcome of who had died (e.g. ruler, queen, etc.) and who was to be entombed with the deceased (e.g. maidservant, musician, groom, etc.), then this logic had to be embedded in the routine workings of those institutional households that defined queens and maidservants in the first place. However, two details of Pollock's argument seem problematic; namely her insistence on the elite nature of the attendants buried in the tombs and her narrow focus on banquets as the primary context for formation of the 'docile bodies' of the attendants.

One problem for Pollock's assumption that the dead of the Royal Cemetery 'held ritual/cultic or managerial posts' (Pollock 2007a: 99) within an institutional household is the evidence for heavy, task specific, skeletal modifications suggested by Molleson and Hogson (1993; 2000; 2003: 125–7) in their study of a limited number of surviving skeletons from the Royal Tombs. Pollock (2007b: 214n. 4) rejects their conclusions as exaggerated, pointing to the sampling problems I have noted above. However, even if the osteological evidence for extreme manual labour on the part of the buried attendant is problematic, it is interesting that the roles in which these bodies have been cast within the Royal Tombs are to a large extent the roles of service emphasised in Early Dynastic banquet scenes. Musicians, grooms, soldiers and maidservants are the supporting cast of both the Royal Tombs and the banquet scenes. If we accept recent evidence (Baadsgaard et al. 2011) that at least some of the attendants' deaths were violently assisted by blows to the head, then the question of who was included in the Royal Tombs and why becomes rather problematic. I think that Pollock is correct in asserting that burial in the Royal Cemetery was selective and based on one's position within an institutional household. However, the nature of such households was quite complex, as was the composition of their dependent membership. Understanding how some members of these households were constituted as 'killable subjects' requires us to go beyond banquets as public expressions of those households, not least because the step from the table to the tomb is a rather large one. Instead, we need to examine the economic and political relationships that defined households and dependency in the Early Dynastic period.

Early Dynastic archives from ancient Girsu (modern Telloh) and Šuruppak (modern Fara) give us some insight into such relations of dependency. The archive at Girsu belonged to a large institutional household headed by the Queen of Lagash. The archives at Šuruppak seem to have been produced by two institutional households ('the palace' and 'the house of the city') of uncertain relation (*cf.* Visicato 1995 and Cripps 2007), both of which may have been headed by the same governor. At the core of these institutional archives was the routine (usually monthly) disbursement of rations (barley, oil and wool) on the part of the large, land-holding households to a variety of individuals (e.g. Gelb 1965; Maekawa 1973/4). It is also clear that not all residents of either Girsu or Šuruppak received rations from the institutional households in question. Giuseppe Visicato (1995: 25–6) has estimated the number of dependants of the 'palace' in Šurruppak as 2,500–3,000 based on the number of its administrative sub-divisions and their average membership. At Girsu, actually documented recipients of rations range between 428 and 697 individuals per year, although only an estimated 30 per cent of this archive has survived (see Prentice 2010: 20, 65 and 79). Both Tell Fara (ancient Šurruppak) and Telloh (ancient Girsu) are *tells* of ca. 100 hectares in area, and hence their populations can be estimated at perhaps 10,000–25,000 residents. So, the direct dependants of what appear to have been the primary institutions at Šurruppak and Girsu would have represented a sizable minority of the population.

At the broadest level, both the Girsu and Šuruppak archives distinguish two ways in which people were attached to these large institutional households as dependants (see Cripps 2007; Prentice 2010). In the first category are people who have been given land allotments for personal use by an institutional household. In return they were required to perform some kind of service to that institution, usually manual labour (such as canal digging and harvesting) or military service (Cripps 2007; Maekawa 1973/4). Tablets show that at both Girsu and Šurruppak people in this category received barley rations for only part of the year, apparently while fulfilling their labour service requirements. It is not clear whether all such persons fulfilled these labour obligations themselves, or whether some may have organised and supplied workers from their own dependants who were then fed by the institution's barley rations during the period of labour service (see Prentice 2010: 74–82).

In the second category are people who received barley rations every month, all year round, from the stores of the institutional household in question (see Prentice 2010; Visicato 1995). These involve people categorised by a wide variety of professional titles covering labourers, craftspersons and priestly and domestic staff. The distinction between those receiving monthly rations all year round and those with land grants is not marked by profession. Indeed, members of at least 14 professions (e.g. cooks, cupbearers, leather workers, boatmen, shepherds, smiths, etc.) are found in both categories at Girsu (Prentice 2010: 72). However, there does seem to be a distinction in rank, since approximately half of the individuals named on ration lists for those given land grants reappear on the other rations lists as supervisors of those receiving monthly rations (Prentice 2010: 72). At both Šurruppak (Visicato1995) and Girsu (Prentice 2010) it is evident that the receipt of rations is mediated by supervisors defined according to profession, who are responsible for mustering and directing dependant labour in exchange for special consideration such as land grants. At Girsu it would also appear that such supervisors were provided with the means of production (e.g. tools, raw material) and assigned quotas by the Queen's household with the possibility of accumulating debts or surplus in relation to the institution (Magid 2001: 323–4). Interestingly, Glenn Magid (2001) has pointed to evidence from Girsu suggesting that some craftworkers on continuous monthly rations may have lacked their own immediate households and lived with their supervisors in what might be termed dependent workshops.

In contrast to the situation with craft-workers, whose relations to the palace or temple – not to mention their basic living conditions – may have been mediated by their immediate supervisors, at both Šurruppak and Girsu there are categories of people receiving continuous monthly rations described as 'belonging to' or 'registered at' the palace (*šà-dub-é-gal*). Such people are usually listed by profession and these professions are what one would expect of a large domestic staff – cooks, cupbearers, messengers, 'inner room', 'store room' and 'hot water' attendants, scribes, hairdressers, cleaners, etc. They also replicate some of the occupations depicted in banquet scenes and represented among the attendant burials in the Royal Tombs. While they too had supervisors, one suspects that some of these people were direct dependants of the palace, in the sense of belonging to no other household, or possessing no other means of subsistence.

Focusing for a moment on those who seem most dependent on institutional households, it is evident that at least some such labourers were unfree. There is textual evidence from Girsu suggesting that some low-status workers were sold to the Queen of Lagash by their overseers (Prentice 2010: 144, 147–8). One might point out that the two sales documents in question involve workers called *igi-nu-du$_8$* ('the blind'), a category of very low-status dependants who usually worked under the supervision of gardeners, and indeed were here sold by gardeners in both texts. A common explanation for this term is that these were prisoners of war who were intentionally blinded and enslaved (Gelb 1973). This may well be the case, however; such transactions were not unique, with other sales documents indicating that *gala* (lamentation singers) as well as a 'foundling' were also sold to the Queen of Lagash, although here the sellers were their parents/ guardians, hence this may have some relation to debt bondage (Prentice 2010: 147–8). Amongst low status textile workers, classified on ration lists as *gemé-dumu* ('women and children'), one finds some referred to as 'purchased' (Prentice 2010: 55–9). This is not to imply that all dependant workers at Girsu were interchangeable chattels of the 'house of the woman/goddess Ba'u'. At Girsu there is also evidence for differential ration rates that seem to relate to worker experience and/or skill (Prentice 2010: 91–5), while amongst female weavers some were promoted over time from weavers to overseers (Prentice 2010: 54–5).

It seems that, within these institutional households, resource allocation and labour obligations both incorporated class relations (e.g. between full-time dependants and supervisors, who held land grants and perhaps also partial control over the means of production and the products of labour) and masked them within an overall ideology of obligatory service by all. To quote Susan Pollock:

> Ideologically, the notion that people of all social stations – and even the gods – received rations may have contributed to a sense that everyone was 'in it together,' that everyone participated in laboring for the common good and received remuneration according to their contribution. (Pollock 2003: 32)

Put simply, the textual evidence from Early Dynastic Sumer suggests that a significant proportion of the population was connected in some way to the large institutional households through networks of dependency. However, the degree, regularity and implications of this dependency varied considerably. Some people came into irregular contact with temple or palace households, perhaps through occasional public works programmes (like canal digging) or indirectly through their relations with local elites. In essence, they lived independently but in the wake of the economic power of temples and palaces. Others were granted the means of production by these institutions, in the form of land, raw materials and perhaps even the allocation of dependent labour. Such persons appear to have been free to accumulate their own wealth once they had met certain obligations to the granting institution. Still others had no independent household of their own, nor any independent means of subsistence; indeed some were officially chattels, in the sense of being purchased by the institution. For those on the domestic staffs of palaces and temples, this may have meant direct dependency on the principal elites of these institutions, for whom they performed a variety of domestic tasks. Such tasks likely included the feeding, attending to and entertaining of elites and their guests, much as was represented in banquet scenes and in the Royal Tombs of Ur.

Banquet scenes were celebratory scenes, just as banquets themselves were celebratory events. They revelled in the abundance produced by institutional households, realised along chains of obligation and command linking dependant workers to human rulers and ultimately to the gods themselves. This was a hegemonic representation of 'the good life' in Early Dynastic Sumer, yet it was also one that, in the extreme case of the Royal Tombs, made imaginable the ritual killing of hundreds of people.

The philosopher Giorgio Agamben (1998; 2005) has argued that the arbitrary foundation of the modern state's power is revealed when exercised in supposed exceptions to the rule of law, such as in states of emergency or in cases that create ambiguous legal identities (e.g. concentration camps, detention of illegal immigrants, the 'enemy combatants' of Guantanamo Bay). These 'states of exception' highlight the ability of the state to exercise coercive power outside of its own legal frameworks, and thereby they undermine the normative assumption that state rule derives in the first instance from law rather than force. Agamben is particularly interested in the manifestation of state power as biopower in Foucault's sense of the shaping, containing and excluding of physical existence, what Agamben describes as 'the politicization of bare life' (Agamben 1998: 6).

Like modern 'states of exception', the extremity of the Royal Tombs of Ur does reveal a particular species of biopower at work in the constitution of institutional households in the third millennium BC However, here 'bare life' is revealed by inclusion in, rather than exclusion from, the state. In the Royal Tombs the very existence of the attendants (their identity, their kinship, their past and their future) was swallowed up by the ritual drama of the funerary banquet. Within the Royal Tombs, the attendants' bodies have no independent referent, they are stripped to the bare facts of their biological life, and once this has been done that life proves easy to extinguish. This was a spectacle in the purest sense: unusual, extreme, overwhelming, laden with messages of order, power, aspiration and fear. Yet, I would argue that this spectacle was imaginable because it had already been constituted in the routine workings of institutional households; regularised through the organisational structure of institutional accounting, the distribution of rations and the management of labour. The existence of people without independent households and without independent means of subsistence, people whose labour could be freely expropriated as a condition of their remaining alive, was both materially and symbolically central to the reproduction of institutional households. 'Killable subjects' were not formed only on the plane of ideology and spectacle. The spectacle of the Royal Tombs was made possible by the material interdependence of institutions, attached labour, production and rations, all articulated within a hegemonic order of universal obligatory service.

We do not know for certain if the attendants buried in the Royal Tombs originated from amongst the household's most dependent members. We do not know if they were loyal and honoured volunteers, prisoners of war, destitute or merely surplus to purpose. What we do know is that, within the funerary spectacle of the Royal Tombs of Ur, such distinctions ceased to matter. Regardless of their origins, those going to their deaths were subsumed into roles of service, replicating the hegemonic order of institutional households in a ritual drama that fused authority, violence and transcendence into sovereignty. Played out in these funerary spectacles was an order in which each gave service according to his or her station. For some this meant offering libations to the gods, for others it meant giving time or barley, and for some it meant a narrow-bladed axe in the back of the head.

7

Conclusion

The hazardous necessity of comparison

I have often found that Angels have the vanity to speak of themselves as the only wise; this they do with a confident insolence sprouting from systematic reasoning.

William Blake, *The Marriage of Heaven and Hell*

As a child I read many more comic books than I care to admit. Yet, despite my familiarity with the genre, it came as a revelation that the seemingly solid colours on the page were actually an effect created by thousands of tiny dots. What I had taken to be a simple case of colouring between the lines turned out to be something rather more mysterious, if only for its ability to hide in plain sight. From that point on, the seemingly solid images of comic books shifted in and out of focus, as I alternately forgot and remembered the lesson of their composition as clouds of coloured dots.

This experience of images that became solid or dissolved depending upon how well I remembered the realities of their composition provides a good analogy for the focus and purpose of this book. As noted in Chapter 1, what we call the state is an effect, rather than an entity; its solidity and the smoothness of its surfaces depends directly on our forgetting the practices, strategies and technologies through which this state-effect is constituted. A large part of this book has been about keeping this state-effect in view, crossing our eyes, as it were, in order to see clouds of dots instead of solid shapes.

This focus is narrower than and rather different from what is usually discussed in literature on the archaeology of the state. Normally, debates focus on the existence and variability of a *bauplan* of the state as an institutional structure shared by distinct entities, whether this be in terms of specialised decision making, resource allocation, dispute resolution, the monopolisation of force, or all of the above. To stretch my comic book analogy, these discussions are primarily about comparing the pictures on the page, while taking for granted their solidly coloured surfaces. In contrast, I have focused on the gestalt experience of seeing pictures on a page composed of dots. Although I have, in this way, raised critical question regarding the reality of the state as a universal entity, I have also explored what I believe to be a real phenomenon involving the intersection of authority, force and transcendence.

With some modification (see Chapter 1), this book can, therefore, be seen as an example of what Adam Smith (2011) has termed 'archaeologies of sovereignty'. Here I understand sovereignty to be the effect of the intersection of authority, force and transcendence, and hegemony to be the condition that allows this intersection to occur. This perspective differs from archaeologies of the state, in that it seeks always to disaggregate and disassemble sovereignty in order to keep visible how it is made. At the same time, it differs from both particularist and deconstructivist positions in that it recognises a general phenomenon that can be fruitfully discussed in relation to a number of distinct cultural and historical contexts.

This last point raises rather directly the problem of comparison. To be clear, the issue is not comparison *per se*, in that comparison is always necessary if we are to have knowledge rather than endlessly discrete sense impressions. What really matters is how, what and why we are comparing; in other words, what do we hold to be comparable, and what do we hope to gain from making such comparisons?

The first question is perhaps the most straightforward, namely the question of comparative method. In this book I have engaged in what Smith and Peregrine would term 'intensive comparison' (Smith and Peregrine 2012), in the sense that I have focused on contextual detail across a limited number of cases. Smith and Peregrine contrast this approach with what they term 'systematic comparison', meaning the statistical analysis of a limited number of attributes across a large number of cases (Smith and Peregrine 2012). This distinction is a long-standing one in anthropology where, for example, it appears in Claude Lévi-Strauss's discussion of the comparative method as it relates to mechanical and statistical models of social structure (Lévi-Strauss 1967: 279–81). Lévi-Strauss (1967: 281) argued that, because cultural variables are never identical across ethnographic contexts, large-scale comparisons are not really very good comparisons at all. Hence, an anthropologist must choose 'either to study many cases in a superficial and in the end ineffective way; or to limit oneself to a thorough study of a small number of cases, thus proving that in the last analysis one well done experiment is sufficient to make a demonstration' (Lévi-Strauss 1967: 281). Yet, as Caspar Bruun Jensen (2011: 5) notes, Lévi-Strauss's search for the 'golden event' that is both a single case and a general demonstration presents an intractable problem: how does one identify a 'golden event' without already knowing what it demonstrates? Certainly this is no less of a problem than that of comparing multiple cases of not-quite-the-same-thing.

In part, at least, the problem lies in what one hopes to achieve by means of comparative study. In this book, I have been much concerned with generalising arguments. For example, I have suggested that transcendence is paired with violence in the constitution of sovereignty through the need to overcome constraints on the legitimate use of force that are general and integral to human collectives. I have also suggested that hegemony demonstrates a general pattern of appropriating, transforming and reinscribing the cultural resources of 'common sense' as the basis for consent in given political regimes. However, unlike Claude Lévi-Strauss and Michael E. Smith, I have not offered these generalisations in order to reveal universal principles in themselves. For example, I am not concerned to extract the abstract principles of political power that structure diverse historical contexts, as if universal significance was demonstrated by the removal of historical content. Rather, I have developed general arguments for the express purpose of re-immersing them in specific historical contexts. In this sense, my generalisations are less models to be tested than tools to facilitate comparative discussions without sacrificing cultural and historical detail. It is for this reason that my use of 'intensive comparison' is particularly important to my goals, as my case studies are meant to develop key concepts through continual re-immersion into the historical and cultural details of specific contexts. This in turn, I hope, will stimulate on-going discussions across specific contexts, but also by means of those contexts, in order to develop, modify and challenge the general concepts I have presented in this book.

So, my goal in working comparatively is to generate dialogues across specific contexts on the common processes of sovereignty for the purpose of both understanding the past and acting in the present. But can one actually do this? Does the presumption of common themes and common analytical concepts not subordinate these different pasts by universalizing a very particular present (twenty-first century, Euro-American, academic)? In other words, is my analytical framework not itself a form of hegemony? At a time when teleological universal histories of political organisation are both popular and abundant (e.g. Diamond 1997; Fukuyama 2011), it seems important to ask if comparative study can indeed take any other form. Here we would do well to consider the unlikely figure of anthropologist Louis Dumont.

Dumont famously (or infamously) framed the study of India in terms of an ideology in which hierarchy (in the form of ritual purity), as a shared value separable from power, served to encompass opposition and thereby constitute a coherent social whole (see Dumont 1980). The specifics of Dumont's interpretation of India have been subject to extensive critique, many of which have been recently reprinted (Khare 2006). Our concern is not so much with these details as with what Dumont saw as both the purpose and the implications of his work. Dumont's anthropology was unabashedly comparative. However, for Dumont the purpose of comparison was not to track similarities but to highlight differences, and to do this not as an act of cross-cultural translation, but rather as a form of ideological auto-critique (Dumont 1975). In other words, the outcome of noting the difference between an Indian emphasis on collectivism and hierarchy and a Western emphasis on individualism and egalitarianism was as much to highlight the ideological nature of Western frames of reference as it was to understand the 'exotic' nature of Indian thought.

As some scholars have noted (e.g. Kapferer 2011), it is in this last regard that Dumont's work finds parallels in the more recent 'ontological turn' within anthropology (e.g. Descola 2006; Viveiros De Castro 2004). For example, Eduardo Viveiros De Castro (2004) has argued that the classic anthropological move of rendering apparently irrational indigenous understandings of the nature of existence (ontology) rational by explaining them as coherent alternate views of a single shared world ('one world, many worldviews') implicitly subordinates these ontologies to our own. As he writes, '[de]scribing this world as if it were an illusory version of our own, unifying the two via a reduction of one to the conventions of the other, is to imagine an overly simple form of relations between them' (Viveiros De Castro 2004: 14). Instead, in a manner similar to Dumont, Viveiros De Castro argues that '[a] good translation is one that allows the alien concepts to deform and subvert the translator's conceptual toolbox …' (Viveiros De Castro 2004: 5). Hence, the purpose of comparison is to encounter and reflect on alterity; indeed, according to Viveiros De Castro (2004: 11), '[s]ince it is only worth comparing the incommensurable, comparing the commensurable is a task for accountants, not anthropologists'.

From such a perspective, my attempts to reflect on premodern political formations by means of concepts derived from the critical analysis of the modern state may have the appearance of accountancy masquerading as anthropology. Dumont in particular might have seen in both my emphasis on the composite nature of sovereignty and my focus on conflict, force and power, the ideology of possessive individualism that he argued has dominated Western social thought since the Enlightenment (Dumont 1986). My attempts to 'look behind the mask' of political power are cast in terms that are unlikely to have been meaningful to those living in the historical contexts I purport to explain. Indeed, my generalising arguments (about sovereignty, hegemony, violence, etc.) risk reducing the specific conventions of these contexts to further examples of my own conventions, rather than allowing them to 'deform and subvert' my 'conceptual toolbox'.

In response, it is important to stress the place of both violence and hegemony in my arguments. The cases analysed in this book are defined by violence. In other words, violence is not a trait ascribed to some other phenomenon such as the state; rather, this book is about sovereignty as a particular species of institutional violence. My observations apply only to the degree that this species of institutional violence occurs in any given context.

The centrality of violence to sovereignty so defined means that conflict and resistance are already embedded in the cases that I have chosen to study. Hence, these contexts do not confront us as a coherent 'Other'; they are already divided by unequal access to the means of violence. Here the meta-cultural status of hegemony becomes important. Hegemony is a totalising project; it aims to exclude or subordinate alternate views. However, hegemony is not itself a totality. As argued in Chapter Two, hegemonic projects select cultural resources from amongst the many possibilities generated by everyday life and configure these resources in the interests of sovereignty. Hence, alternate or excluded configurations can always take shape within a single cultural formation. In other words, the critical analysis of sovereignty is not the exclusive domain of an external, objectivist, unmasking of power. Internal critiques of sovereignty are always possible, critiques that may well draw on the same cultural world and the same ontological assumptions that form the basis of a given hegemonic project. We saw this in Chapter Three in the case of Imerina, where conflict over Radama I's haircut and collective burial rituals saw royals and non-royals configuring the same cultural values in different ways and towards different ends.

Let us consider once again the issue of slavery in Classical Athens. In Book I of *The Politics* Aristotle makes the ontological argument that some human beings are slaves by nature. I suspect that most readers of this book would find Aristotle's views unacceptable; they are also incommensurate with the concept of equality under the law that underpins, amongst other things, the *Universal Declaration of Human Rights* and the legal systems of most modern liberal democracies. In this context, explaining Aristotle's arguments historically or culturally would amount to an act of anthropological 'translation': a means of understanding Aristotle without conceding any truth to his beliefs on the nature of slaves. One might find Aristotle interesting, but one would never doubt that he was wrong.

Aristotle's unacceptable understanding of natural slaves is precisely the kind of alterity that Viveiros de Castro admonishes anthropologists to encounter rather than translate; except for one thing. The way in which Aristotle frames his argument makes it clear that his views were not shared by all of his ancient Greek contemporaries, even if these opposing positions are not well attested in the surviving literature (see Cambiano 1987). Hence, one cannot encounter the alterity of *the* (as in singular) ancient Greek perspective on the nature of slaves without reducing and essentialising the diversity of views that existed at the time of Aristotle (*cf.* Lloyd 2010: 208–9). There is no 'ancient Greek model' to be given priority over our comparative themes and analytical concepts. Indeed, to some extent, we are simply entering into the debate. But this is not really the crux of the matter.

In Plato's *Republic*, Socrates suggests that a rich slave-owner did not live in fear of his slaves because, if they rose up, the whole city would come to the aid of each private citizen. However,

> … if this one man with his fifty or more slaves were lifted out of the city by some god, together with his wife and children, and deposited with his slaves and other property in a deserted place where no free man could come to his assistance, how frightened would he be on his own behalf and that of his wife and children lest they be killed by the slaves? – Very frightened indeed! (Plato, *Republic*, IX.578e)

While he disagrees with Plato on many things, here Aristotle sees the same danger in so far as he deems it necessary to consider measures to prevent slave revolt in discussing the planning of an ideal agrarian landscape (Aristotle, *The Politics*, VII.x.1330a).

Whether or not one viewed slavery as a natural state, slave resistance was clearly thinkable: something for rich men to fear and against which freemen were prepared to mobilise. Hence, the point is not simply that there was a diversity of opinion on the nature of slaves in ancient Athens, but rather that slavery itself, as a relationship of violence, represented a fault-line within Athenian society, one that ran through indigenous perspectives on politics, citizenship, labour or wealth.

Comparing these sorts of fault-lines in different societies is one way in which the comparison of similarities can play a key critical role that goes beyond the imposition of the present onto the past. On issues such as citizenship and slavery in ancient Athens, where the terrain was divided by relations of violence and where the means of self-representation were unequally distributed, comparison can provide us with terms of reference (e.g. sovereignty, hegemony, etc.) distinct from those generated by the powerful in the past. Comparing fault-lines in different contexts also reminds us that there are always people on either side of these social and political divides, highlighting the need to seek out traces of those who have been excluded or forgotten. Returning to our comic book analogy, comparing fault-lines in different contexts helps to make dots visible where one might otherwise have seen only solid colours. In this way, comparison is essential to the critical study of sovereignty.

The benefits of comparison do not exist only for the past; indeed quite the opposite is true. Hence, the comparison of fault-lines is as relevant to modern liberal democracies as it is to ancient Athens or the kingdom of Imerina. For example, equality under the law may be a founding principal to most liberal democratic states, but this principal is also configured in particular ways involving relations of violence that we often forget or take for granted. Equality under the law is linked to citizenship and territory, which define where and to whom the law applies. Citizenship and territory are in turn linked to collective identity and national pride, but they are also linked to mandatory birth registration, residency permits, immigration criteria based upon wealth and education, the presentation of passports, the policing of borders, and the arrest and forcible deportation of 'illegal' non-citizens. Equality under the law is also linked to policing and law enforcement, which in turn entails (amongst other things) the legitimate application of force against citizens (and others). As we all know, equality under the law does not result in the actual equality of citizens. Indeed, in most liberal democracies with a capitalist economy, the law acts to favour some forms of equality (e.g. equality in the right to own property and in the protection of property) against other forms of equality (e.g. equality in the distribution of property), with police and judicial powers deployed to ensure that this is the case. At the same time, citizenship and territory define when the application of force is a police matter and when it is a military matter; in other words when force is applied by the state within the law and when it is projected outside of the law. Furthermore, in states of emergency the law itself can be suspended for the purposes of preserving or rescuing the law and the institutions of democracy, when these are viewed to be under threat from, for example, terrorism or insurrection.

These many relationships of violence may well be necessities of living in large-scale communities; the price of liberty, as some would have it. Yet, in comparative perspective these unfortunate necessities begin to look somewhat different. For example, the maintenance of order, and the continuation of a particular mode of life, were as important to Egyptian Pharaohs and Inca Emperors as they are to the politicians and citizens of modern liberal democracies. Indeed, as I hope this book has shown, there are many grounds for comparison in this regard. The difference, many will say, lies in the content of what is being defended and the manner and limits placed on this defence; but this is exactly my point.

The relationships of institutional violence that we perpetuate are not simply unfortunate necessities of complex polities; they represent a choice regarding what forms of order and what modes of life we deem worthy of preservation and at what cost. Comparative study does not make this choice for us, but it does make clear that a choice is being made; it requires us to ask: 'what exactly are we defending and why?' It requires us to recognise the hegemonic projects within which we are embedded and to ask whose interests are being perpetuated and to what ends? We may be happy to find that the interests are our own and that our consent is freely given; but even this should arise from critical reflection and not from virtual relations that we take for granted.

To my mind, open and informed discussion of such issues holds a greater potential to 'subvert and deform' our 'conceptual toolbox' than does an exclusive focus on the alterity of the past. In this sense, a comparative archaeology of sovereignty has a role to play in stimulating reflection, debate and action on how we live together in the world. We could, and many do, pursue this role like one of William Blake's angels, speaking of ourselves as 'the only wise' and producing teleological histories of the world as we already know it to be. The more difficult and rewarding task is to embrace the devil in the contextual detail, thinking comparatively while allowing ourselves to be challenged by the diverse possibilities of human existence. This is the task that I set myself in writing this book, one that could only ever be imperfectly realised given the limits of time and my own personal abilities. Yet such imperfection has its place if it opens the door to future, better informed, discussions regarding political power and human diversity from a long-term perspective. After a decade of war, terror and crisis, such discussions are certainly needed. What form they take and what action they engender will depend, at least in part, on decisions made by people like you, the readers of this book.

Bibliography

Adam, S. (2007) Response á Edward Harris. In *Symposion 2005: Vorträge zur griechischen und hellenistischen Rechtsgeschichte.* Austrian Academy of Sciences: Vienna; 177–82.

Adams, A. and J. Brady (2005) Ethnographic notes on Maya Q'eqchi' cave rites: implications for archaeological interpretation. In Brady, J. and K. Prufer (eds), *In the maw of the earth monster: Mesoamerican ritual cave use.* University of Texas Press: Austin, TX; 302–27.

Abrams, P. (1988) Notes on the difficulty of studying the state (1977). *Journal of Historical Sociology* 1(1): 58–89.

Agamben, G. (1998) *Homo Sacer: Sovereign power and bare life.* Trans. D. Heller-Roazan. Stanford University Press: Palo Alto, CA.

—(2005) *State of exception.* Trans. K. Attell. University of Chicago Press: Chicago.

Alberti Manzanares, P. (1986) Una institución exclusivamente femenina en la época incaica: las acilacuna. *Revista Española de Antropología Americana* 16: 153–90.

Algaze, G. (1983–4) Private houses and graves at Ingharra, a reconsideration. *Mesopotamia* 18–19: 135–91.

Alonso, A. (1994) The politics of space, time and substance: state formation, nationalism, and ethncity. *ARA* 23: 379–405.

Amiet, P. (1980) *La glyptique mésopotamienne archaïque.* 2nd edn. Editions du centre national de la recherche scientifique: Paris.

Anderson, G. (2009) The personality of the Greek State. *Journal of Hellenic Studies* 129: 1–22.

Aristotle (1962) *The Politics.* Trans. J. Sinclair. Penguin Classics. Harmondsworth.

Baadsgaard A., J. Monge, S. Cox and R. Zettler (2011) Human sacrifice and intentional corpse preservation in the Royal Cemetery of Ur. *Antiquity* 85: 27–42.

Baadsgaard, A., J. Monge and R. Zettler (2012) Bludgeoned, burned, and beautified: re-evaluating mortuary practices in the Royal Cemetery of Ur. In A. Porter and G. Schwartz (eds), *Sacred killing: The archaeology of sacrifice in the ancient Near East.* Eisenbrauns: Winona Lake, IN; 125–58.

Baines, J. and N. Yoffee (1998) Order, legitimacy and wealth in Ancient Egypt and Mesopotamia. In Feinman, G. and J. Marcus (eds), *Archaic states*. SAR Press: Santa Fe, NM: 199–260.

—(2000) Order, legitimacy, and wealth: setting the terms. In Richards, J. and M. Van Buren (eds), *Order, legitimacy, and wealth in ancient states*. Cambridge University Press: Cambridge; 13–17.

Bartelson, J. (2001) *The critique of the State*. Cambridge University Press: Cambridge.

Barrett, J. and I. Ko (2009) A phenomenology of landscape: a crisis in British landscape archaeology? *Journal of Social Archaeology* 9(3): 275–94.

Bauer, B. (1996) Legitimization of the state in Inca myth and ritual. *AA* 98(2): 327–37.

Bauer, B. and R. A. Covey (2002) Processes of state formation in the Inca heartland (Cuzco, Peru). *AA* 104(3): 846–64.

Beld, S. (2002) The *Queen of Lagash: Ritual economy in a Sumerian state*. Unpublished Ph.D. dissertation. University of Michigan: Ann Arbor, MI.

Belrose-Huyghues, V. (1983) Structure et symbolique de l'espace royal en Imerina. In F. Raison-Jourdes (ed.), *Les Souverains de Madagascar: L'histoire royale et ses resurgences contemporaines*. Éditions Karthala: Paris; 125–52.

Berent, M. (2000) Anthropology and the Classics: war, violence, and the stateless *polis*. *CQ* 50(1): 257–89.

—(2006) The stateless *polis*: a reply to critics. *SEH* 5(1): 141–63.

Berg, G. (1981) Riziculture and the founding of monarchy in Imerina. *The Journal of African History* 22: 289–308.

—(1985) The sacred musket: tactics, technology and power in eighteenth century Madagascar. *CSSH* 27: 261–79.

Bintliff, J. (2006) Solon's reforms: an archaeological perspective. In Blok, J. and A. Lardinois (eds), *Solon of Athens: New historical and philological approaches*. Mnemosyne, Bibliotheca Classica Batava Supplementum. Brill: Leiden; 321–33.

Blanton, R. (1998) Beyond centralization: steps toward a theory of egalitarian behavior in Archaic States. In Feinman, G., and J. Marcus (eds), *Archaic states*. SAR Press: Santa Fe, NM; 135–72.

Blanton, R. and L. Fargher (2008) *Collective action in the formation of pre-modern states*. Springer: New York.

Bloch, M. (1971) *Placing the dead: Tombs, ancestral villages, and kinship organization in Madagascar.* Waveland Press Inc.: London.

—(1986) *From blessing to violence: History and ideology in the circumcision ritual of the Merina of Madagascar.* Cambridge University Press: Cambridge.

—(1987) The ritual of the royal bath in Madagascar: the dissolution of death, birth and fertility into authority. In D. Cannadine (ed.), *Rituals of royalty: Power and ceremonial in traditional socieities.* Cambridge University Press: Cambridge; 271-97.

Blok, J. and A. Lardinois (eds) (2006) *Solon of Athens: New historical and philological approaches.* Mnemosyne, Bibliotheca Classica Batava Supplementum. Brill: Leiden.

Boese, J. (1971) *Altmesopotamische Weihplatten: Eine sumerische Denkmalsgattung des 3. Jahrtausends v. Chr.* De Gruyter: Berlin.

Bourdieu, P. (1999) Rethinking the State: genesis and structure of the bureaucratic field. In G. Steinmetz (ed.), *State/Culture: State formation after the cultural turn.* Cornell University Press: Ithaca, NY; 53-75.

Brady, J. (1997) Settlement configuration and cosmology: the role of caves at Dos Pilas. *AA* 99(3): 602-18.

Brady, J. and W. Ashmore (1999) Mountains, caves, water: ideational landscapes of the Ancient Maya. In W. Ashmore and A. B. Knapp (eds), *Archaeologies of landscape: Contemporary perspectives.* Blackwell Publishing: Oxford; 124-45.

Brady, J. and K. Prufer (eds) (2005) *In the maw of the earth monster: Mesoamerican ritual cave use.* University of Texas Press: Austin, TX.

Bray, T. (2003) Inka pottery as culinary equipment: food, feasting, and gender in imperial state design. *LAA* 14(1): 3-28.

—(2009) The role of *chicha* in Inca state expansion: a distributional study of Inca *aríbalos.* In Jennings, J. and B. Bowser (eds), *Power, drink and society in the Andes.* University Press of Florida: Gainesville, FL; 108-32.

Brock, R. (1994) The labour of women in Classical Athens. *CQ* 44(2): 336-46.

Brück, J. (2005) Experiencing the past? The development of a phenomenological archaeology in British prehistory. *AD* 12(1): 45-72.

Brumfiel, E. (1992) Distinguished lecture in archaeology: Breaking and entering the ecosystem – gender, class and faction steal the show. *AA* 94(3): 551-67.

Brumfiel, E. and T. Earle (eds) (1987) *Specialization, exchange and complex societies.* Cambridge University Press: Cambridge.

Bruun Jensen, C. (2011) Comparative relativism: symposium on an impossibility. *Common Knowledge* 17(1): 1–12.

Burford, A. (1993) *Land and labor in the Greek world.* The Johns Hopkins University Press: Baltimore.

Callet, F. (ed.) (1908) *Tantara ny Adriana eto Madagascar: Documents historiques d'après les manuscrits malgaches.* 2 vols. Académie Malgache: Tananarive.

Cambiano, G. (1987) Aristotle and the anonymous opponents of slavery. *Slavery and Abolition* 8(1): 22–41.

Campbell, G. (2005) *An economic history of imperial Madagascar, 1750–1895.* Cambridge University Press: Cambridge.

Campbell, R. (2008) Comments on Flad (2008). *CA* 49(3): 420–1.

Cartledge, P., E. Cohen and L. Foxhall (eds) (2002) *Money, labour and land: Approaches to the economies of ancient Greece.* Routledge: London.

Chang, K.-C. (1983) *Art, myth and ritual: The path to political authority in ancient China.* Cambridge University Press: Cambridge, MA.

Chapman, R. (2003) *Archaeologies of Complexity.* Routledge: London.

Child, M. (2007) Ritual purification and the ancient Maya sweatbath at Palenque. In D. Marken (ed.), *Palenque: Recent investigations at the Classic Maya center.* Altamira Press: Lanham, MD; 233–62.

Clastres, P. (1977) *Society against the State.* Trans. R. Hurley. Urizen Books: New York.

Coggins, C. C. and O. C. Shane (eds) (1984) *Cenote of sacrifice: Maya treasures from the Sacred Well at Chichén Itzá.* University of Texas Press: Austin TX.

Cohen, A. (2005) *Death rituals, ideology, and the development of early Mesopotamian kingship.* Brill: Leiden.

Cohen, D. (1989) Seclusion, separation, and the status of women in Classical Athens. *Greece and Rome* 36(1): 3–15.

Cohen, E. (2000) *The Athenian nation.* Princeton University Press: Princeton.

—(2002) An unprofitable masculinity. In P. Cartledge, E. Cohen and L. Foxhall (eds) (2002) *Money, labour and land: Approaches to the economies of ancient Greece.* Routledge: London; 100–12.

Comaroff, J. and J. Comaroff (1991) *Of revelation and revolution.* Vol. 1. University of Chicago Press: Chicago.

Connerton, P. (1989) *How societies remember.* Cambridge University Press: Cambridge.

Cooper, J. (1986) *Presargonic inscriptions*. Sumerian and Akkadian royal inscriptions 1. American Oriental Society: New Haven.

Costin, C. (1998) Housewives, chosen women, skilled men: cloth production and social identity in the late Prehispanic Andes. In C. Costin and R. Wright (eds), *Craft and social identity*. APAAA 8. Wiley-Blackwell: Washington, DC; 123–41.

Coucouzeli, A. (2007) From megaron to *oikos* at Zagora. In R. Westgate, N. Fischer and J. Whitley (eds), *Building communities: House, settlement and society in the Aegean and beyond. Proceedings of a conference held at Cardiff University, 17–12 April 2001*. British School at Athens: London; 169–81.

Crehan, K. (2002) *Gramsci, culture and anthropology*. University of California Press: Beskley, CA.

Cripps, E. (2007) *Land tenure and social stratification in ancient Mesopotamia: Third millennium Sumer before the Ur III dynasty*. BAR International series 1676. Archaeopress: Oxford.

Crossland, Z. (2001) Time and the ancestors: landscape survey in the Andrantsay region of Madagascar. *Antiquity* 75: 825–36.

Dahl, R. (1989) *Democracy and its critics*. Yale University Press: New Haven.

D'Altroy, T. (1992) *Provincial power in the Inka Empire*. Smithsonian: Washington, DC.

Davidson, J. (2011) Bodymaps: sexing space and zoning gender in Ancient Athens. *Gender and History* 23(3): 597–614.

Davies, J. (1981) *Wealth and the power of wealth in Classical Athens*. Arno Press: New York.

Davis-Salazar, K. (2003) Late Classic Maya water management and community organization at Copán, Honduras. *LAA* 14(3): 275–99.

—(2006) Late Classic Maya drainage and flood control at Copán, Honduras. *Ancient Mesoamerica* 17: 125–38.

De Mecquenem, R. (1943) *Fouilles de Suse, 1933–1939*. Mémoires de la Mission Archéologique en Iran (Mission de Susiane) 29. Paul Geuthner: Paris.

Demarrais E., L. J. Castillo and T. Earle (1996) Ideology, materialization, and power strategies. *CA* 37(1): 15–31.

Dewar, R. (2007) Processual assessment of population changes in Western Avaradrano. In H. Wright (ed.), *Early state formation in central Madagascar: An archaeological survey of western Avaradrano*. Museum of Anthropology, University of Michigan: Ann Arbor, MI; 101–3.

Diakonoff, I. (1987) Slave-labour vs. non-slave labour: the problem of
    definition. In M. Powell (ed.), *Labor in the ancient Near East.* American
    Oriental Society Series 68. American Oriental Society: New Haven, CT; 1–3.

Diamond, J. (1997) *Guns, germs and steel: A short history of everybody for the
    last 13,000 years.* Vintage: London.

Dickson, D. B. (2006) Public transcripts expressed in theatres of cruelty: the
    Royal Graves at Ur in Mesopotamia. *CAJ* 16(2): 123–44.

Dietler, M. (2001) Theorizing the feast. In M. Dietler and B. Hayden (eds),
    *Feasts: Archaeological and ethnographic perspectives on food, politics and
    power.* Smithsonian: Washington, DC; 87–125.

Dietler, M. and B. Hayden (eds) (2001) *Feasts: Archaeological and ethnographic
    perspectives on food, politics and power.* Smithsonian: Washington, DC.

Dillon, M. (2002) *Girls and women in Classical Greek religion.* Routledge: London.

Dumont, L. (1975) On the comparative understanding of non-modern
    civilizations. *Daedalus* 104(2): 153–72.

—(1980) *Homo hierarchicus: The caste system and its implications.* University
    of Chicago Press: Chicago.

—(1986) *Essays on individualism: Modern ideology in anthropological
    perspective.* University of Chicago Press: Chicago.

Dunnell, R. (1980) Evolutionary theory and archaeology. In M. Schiffer (ed.),
    Advances in Archaeological Method and Theory. Volume 3. Academic
    Press: New York; 38–99.

Dunning, N. and T. Beach (1994) Soil erosion, slope management, and
    ancient terracing in the Maya Lowlands. *LAA* 5(1): 51–69.

Dunning, N., T. Beach, and S. Luzzadder-Beach (2006) Environmental
    variability among bajos in the southern Maya Lowlands and its
    implications for Ancient Maya civilization and archaeology. In L. Lucero
    and B. Fash (eds), *Precolumbian water management: Ideology, ritual and
    power.* University of Arizona Press: Tucson, AZ; 81–99.

Ehrenreich, R., C. Crumely and J. Levy (eds) (1995) *Heterarchy and the
    analysis of complex societies.* APAAA 6. American Anthropological
    Association: Arlington, VA.

Eickhoff, T. (1993) *Grab und Beigabe: Bestattungssitten der Nekropole von
    Tall Ahmad al-Hattū und anderer frühdynastischer Begräbnisstätten im
    südlichen Mesopotamien und in Luristān. Profil Verlag:* München.

Eisenstadt, Sh. (1963) *The political systems of empires.* Transaction Publishers:
    New York.

Ellis, S. (1985) *The rising of the Red Shawls: A revolt in Madagascar 1895–1899.* Cambridge University Press: Cambridge.

Ellison, R., J. Renfrew, D. Brothwell and N. Seeley (1978) Some food offerings from Ur, excavated by Sir Leonard Woolley, and previously unpublished. *Journal of Archaeological Science* 5(2): 167–77.

Fabian, J. (1983) *Time and the other: How anthropology makes its object.* Columbia University Press: New York.

Fash, B. (2005) Iconographic evidence for water management and social organization at Copán. In E. W. Andrews and W. Fash (eds), *Copán: The history of an ancient Maya kingdom.* SAR Press: Santa Fe, NM; 103–38.

Fash, B. and K. Davis-Salazar (2006) Copán water ritual and management: imagery and sacred place. In L. Lucero and B. Fash (eds), *Precolumbian water management: Ideology, ritual and power.* University of Arizona Press: Tucson, AZ; 129–43.

Feinman, G. and J. Marcus (eds) (1998) *Archaic states.* SAR Press: Santa Fe, NM.

Feng, L. (2008) *Bureaucracy and the state in early China: Governing the Western Zhou.* Cambridge University Press: Cambridge.

Finley, M. (1981) Was Greek civilization based on slave labour? In B. D. Shaw and R. P. Saller (eds), *Economy and society in Ancient Greece.* Penguin Books: London; 97–115.

Flad, R. (2008) Divination and power: a multiregional view of the development of oracle bone divination in Early China. *CA* 49(3): 403–37.

Flannery, K. (1998) The ground plans of archaic states. In G. Feinman and J. Marcus (eds), *Archaic states.* SAR Press: Santa Fe, NM; 15–57.

—(1999) Process and agency in early state formation. *CAJ* 9(1): 3–21.

Flannery, K., J. Marcus and R. Reynolds (2009) *The flocks of the Wamani: A study of llama herders on the punas of Ayacucho, Peru.* Left Coast Press: Walnut Creek, CA.

Forsdyke, S. (2006) Land, labor and economy in Solonian Athens: breaking the impasse between archaeology and history. In J. Blok and A. Lardinois (eds), *Solon of Athens: New historical and philological approaches.* Mnemosyne, Bibliotheca Classica Batava Supplementum. Brill: Leiden; 334–50.

Foucault, M. (1977) *Discipline and punish: The birth of the prison.* Vintage: New York.

—(2007) *Security, territory and population: Lectures at the Collège de France, 1977–78.* Trans. G. Burchell. Palgrave Macmillan: Houndsmills.

—(2008) *The birth of biopolitics: Lectures at the Collège de France, 1978–79.* Trans. G. Burchell. Palgrave Macmillan: Houndsmills, UK.

Foxhall, L. (1989) Household, gender and property in Classical Athens. *CQ* 39(1): 22–44.

—(1994) Pandora unbound: a feminist critique of Foucault's *History of Sexuality.* In A. Cornwall and N. Lindisfarne (eds), *Dislocating masculinity: Comparative ethnographies.* Routledge: London; 133–45.

—(2002) Access to resources in classical Greece: the egalitarianism of the *polis* in practice. In P. Cartledge, E. Cohen and L. Foxhall (eds), *Money, labour and land: Approaches to the economies of ancient Greece.* Routledge: London; 209–20.

Frankfort, H. (1948) *Kingship and the gods: A study of ancient Near Eastern religion as the integration of society and nature.* University of Chicago: Chicago.

French, K. (2007) Creating space through water management at the Classic Maya site of Palenque, Chiapas. In D. Marken (ed.), *Palenque: Recent investigations at the Classic Maya center.* Altamira Press: Lanham, MD; 123–32.

French, K., D. Stuart and A. Morales (2006) Archaeological and epigraphic evidence for water ritual and management at Palenque. In L. Lucero and B. Fash (eds), *Precolumbian water management: Ideology, ritual and power.* Tucson, AZ; 144–52.

Fukuyama, F. (2011) *The origins of political order.* Farrar, Strauss and Giroux: London.

Gabler, S. (2007) Entries, gates and discs in Western Avaradrano. In H. Wright (ed.), *Early state formation in central Madagascar: An archaeological survey of western Avaradrano.* Museum of Anthropology, University of Michigan: Ann Arbor, MI; 63–6.

Gabrielsen, V. (1994) *Financing the Athenian fleet: Public taxation and social relations.* The Johns Hopkins University Press: Baltimore.

Gansell, A. (2007) Identity and adornment in the third-millennium BC Mesopotamian 'Royal Cemetery' at Ur. *CAJ* 17(1): 29–46.

Geertz, C. (1980) *Negara: The theatre state in nineteenth century Bali.* Princeton University Press: Princeton.

Gelb, I. (1965) The ancient Mesopotamian ration system. *JNES* 24(3): 230–43.

—(1973) Prisoners of war in early Mesopotamia. *JNES* 32(1–2): 70–98.

Giddens, A. (1985) *The nation-state and violence.* University of California Press: Berkeley, CA.

Glatz, C., A. Kandler and J. Steele (2011) Pottery production in the Hittite capital: Cultural selection and drift in the bowl repertoire. In E. Cochrane and A. Gardner (eds), *Evolutionary and interpretive archaeologies: A discussion.* Left Coast Press: Walnut Creek, CA; 199–226.

Goldwasser, O. (2002) *Prophets, lovers and giraffes – wor[l]d classification in ancient Egypt.* Göttinger Orientforschungen IV. Reihe Ägypten 38. Harrassowitz Verlag: Wiesbaden.

Gose, P. (1993) Segmentary state formation and the ritual control of water under the Incas. *CSSH* 35(3): 480–514.

—(1996) Oracles, divine kingship and political representation in the Inka State. *Ethnohistory* 43(1): 1–32.

—(2000) The State as chosen woman: brideservice and the feeding of tributaries in the Inka Empire. *AA* 102(1): 84–97.

Graeber, D. (2004) *Fragments of an anarchist anthropology.* Prickly Paradigm Press: Chicago.

—(2007) *Lost people: Magic and the legacy of slavery in Madagascar.* Indiana University Press: Bloomington.

Gramsci, A. (1971) *Selections from the prison notebooks of Antonio Gramsci.* Ed and trans. Q. Hoare, and G. Nowell Smith. International Publishers Co.: New York.

—(2000) *The Antonio Gramsci reader: Selected writings 1916–1935.* D. Forgacs (ed.). New York University: New York.

Grinin, L. (2004) Democracy and early state. *SEH* 3(2): 93–147.

Grossberg, L. (1986) On postmodernism and articulation: An interview with Stuart Hall. *Journal of Communication Inquiry* 10: 45–60.

Habermas, J. (1989) *The structural transformation of the public sphere: An inquiry into a category of bourgeois society.* Trans. T. Burger. Cambridge University Press: Cambridge.

Hansen, M. H. (1991) *The Athenian democracy in the age of Demosthenes: Structure, principles and ideology.* Trans. J. A. Cook. Basil Blackwell: Oxford.

—(1998) *Polis and city-state: An ancient concept and its modern equivalent.* Munksgaard: Copenhagen.

Hansen, T. and F. Stepputat (2006) Sovereignty revisited. *ARA* 35: 295–315.

Hanson, V. (1995) *The other Greeks: The family farm and the agrarian roots of Western Civilization.* The Free Press: New York.

Harmansah, Ö. (2007) 'Source of the Tigris'. Event, place and performance in the Assyrian landscapes of the early Iron Age. *AD* 14(2): 179–204.

Harris, E. (2002) Workshop, marketplace and household: the nature of technical specialisation in Classical Athens and its influence on economy and society. In P. Cartledge, E. Cohen and L. Foxhall (eds), *Money, labour and land: Approaches to the economies of ancient Greece.* Routledge: London; 67–99.

—(2007) Who enforced the law in Classical Athens? In *Symposion 2005: Vorträge zur griechischen und hellenistischen Rechtsgeschichte.* Austrian Academy of Sciences: Vienna; 159–76.

Harvey, D. (1985) The geopolitics of capitalism. In D. Gregory and J. Urry (eds), *Social relations and spatial structures.* Palgrave Macmillan: London; 128–63.

Hastorf, C. (1990) The effect of the Inka state on Sausa agricultural production and crop consumption. *American Antiquity* 55(2): 262–90.

Hastorf, C. and S. Johanessen (1993) Pre-Hispanic political change and the role of maize in the central Andes of Peru. *AA* 95(1): 115–38.

Hayden, B. (2001) Fabulous feasts: a prolegomenon to the importance of feasting. In M. Dietler and B. Hayden (eds), *Feasts: Archaeological and ethnographic perspectives on food, politics and power.* Smithsonian: Washington, DC; 23–64.

—(2009) Funerals as feasts: why are they so important? *CAJ* 19(1): 29–52.

Heidegger, M. (1962) *Being and time.* Trans. J. Macquarrie and E. Robinson. Basil Blackwell: Oxford.

Heimpel, W. (1992) Herrentum und Königtum im vor und frühgeschictlichen Alten Orient. *Zeitschrift für Assyriologie und Vorderasiatische Archäologie* 82(1): 4–21.

Hobbes, T. (1985 [1651]) *Leviathan.* Penguin: London.

Hodder, I. (2005) Socialization and feasting at Çatalhöyük: a response to Adams. *American Antiquity* 70(1): 189–91

—(2006) The spectacle of daily performance at Çatalhöyük. In T. Inomata and L. Coben (eds), *Archaeology of performance: Theatres of power, community and politics.* Altamira Press: Lanham, MD; 81–102.

Hooper, R. J. (1953) The Attic silver mines in the fourth century BC *Annual of the British School at Athens* 48: 200–54.

—(1968) The Laurion mines: A reconsideration. *Annual of the British School at Athens* 63: 293–326.

Houston, S. (2006) Impersonation, dance and the problem of spectacle among the Classic Maya. In T. Inomata and L. Coben (eds), *Archaeology of performance: Theatres of power, community and politics.* Altamira Press: Lanham, MD; 135–55.

Hunter, V. (1994) *Policing Athens: Social control in the Attic lawsuits, 420–320 BC* Princeton University Press: Princeton.

Inomata, T. (2004) The spatial mobility of non-elite populations in Classic Maya society and its political implications. In J. C. Lohse and F. Valdez, Jr. (eds), *Ancient Maya commoners.* University of Texas Press: Austin, TX; 175–96.

—(2006) Plazas, performers, and spectators: political theaters of the Classical Maya. *CA* 47(5): 805–42.

Inomata, T. and L. Coben (2006) Overture: an invitation to the archaeological theatre. In T. Inomata and L. Coben (eds), *Archaeology of performance: Theatres of power, community and politics.* Altamira Press: Lanham, MD; 11–44.

Jacobsen, T. (1957) Early political developments in Mesopotamia. *Zeitschrift für Assyriologie und Vorderasiatische Archäologie.* 52(1): 91–140.

Jagersma, B. (2007) The calendar of the funerary cult in ancient Lagash. *Biblotheca Orientalis* 64(3–4): 289–307.

Jameson, M. (1977/78) Agriculture and slavery in Classical Athens. *The Classical Journal* 73(2): 122–45.

—(1990) Domestic space in the Greek city-state. In S. Kent (ed.), *Domestic architecture and the use of space: An interdisciplinary cross-cultural study.* Cambridge University Press: Cambridge; 92–113.

—(1992) Agricultural labor in Ancient Greece. In B. Wells (ed.), *Agriculture in ancient Greece:* proceedings of the seventh international symposium at the Swedish institute at Athens, 16–17 May 1990. Paul Åström: Göteborg; 135–46.

Jay, M. (1984) *Marxism and totality: The adventures of a concept from Lukács to Habermas.* University of California Press: Berkeley, CA.

Jennings, J. (2003) The fragility of imperialist ideology and the end of local traditions, an Inca example. *CAJ* 13(1): 107–20.

—(2004) *La chichera y el patrón*: chicha and the energetics of feasting in the prehistoric Andes. In C. Conlee, D. O. and K. Vaughn (eds), *Foundations of power in the prehispanic Andes.* APAAA 14. American Anthropological Association: Washington, DC; 241–59.

Jennings, J. and B. Bowser (eds) (2009) *Power, drink and society in the Andes.*
    University Press of Florida: Gainesville, FL.

Jennings, J. and M. Chatfield (2009) Pots, brewers and hosts: woman's power
    and the limits of central Andean feasting. In J. Jennings and B. Bowser
    (eds), *Power, drink and society in the Andes.* University Press of Florida:
    Gainesville, FL; 200–31.

Jessop, B. (2006) *Spatial fixes, temporal fixes and spatio-temporal fixes.*
    In N. Castree and D. Gregory (eds), *David Harvey: A critical reader.*
    Blackwell Publishing: Oxford; 142–66.

—(2007) *State power.* Polity Press: Cambridge.

Jing, Zhichun (2008) Comments on Flad (2008). *CA* 49(3): 424–5.

Johnson, M. (2006) Discussion article: On the nature of theoretical
    archaeology and archaeological theory. *AD* 13(2): 117–82.

Johnston, K. (2004) Lowland Maya water management practices: the
    household exploitation of rural wells. *Geoarchaeology* 9(3): 265–92.

Jones, A. (2007) *Memory and material culture.* Cambridge University Press:
    Cambridge.

Joyce, R. (2005) Archaeology of the body. *ARA* 34: 139–58.

Kapferer, B. (2011) Strathern's new comparative anthropology: thoughts from
    Hagen and Zambia. *Common Knowledge* 17(1): 104–10.

Keeley, L. (1996) *War before civilization: The myth of the peaceful savage.*
    Oxford University Press: Oxford.

Kent, R. (1970) *Early kingdoms in Madagascar 1500–1700.* Holt, Rinehart and
    Winston: New York.

Kertzer, D. (1996) *Politics and symbols: The Italian Communist Party and the
    fall of Communism.* Yale University Press: New Haven.

Khare, R. S. (ed.) (2006) *Caste, Hierarchy, and Individualism: Indian Critiques
    of Louis Dumont's Contributions.* Oxford University Press: Oxford.

Kohl, P. (1984) Force, history, and the evolutionist paradigm. In M. Spriggs
    (ed.), *Marxist Perspectives in Archaeology.* Cambridge University Press:
    Cambridge; 127–34.

—(1987) State formation: useful concept or idée fixe? In T. Patterson
    and C. Gailey (eds), *Power relations and state formation.* Sheffield
    Publishing Company: Salem, WI; 27–34.

Kuper, A. (2000) If memes are the answer what is the question? In
    R. Aunger (ed.), *Darwinizing culture: The status of memetics as a science.*
    Oxford University Press: Oxford; 175–88.

Kurtz, D. (1996) Hegemony and anthropology: Gramsci, exegeses, reinterpretations. *Critique of Anthropology* 16(2): 103–35.

—(2006) Political power and government: negating the anthropomorphized state. *SEH* 5(2): 91–111.

Kus, S. (1992) Toward an archaeology of body and soul. In J.-C. Gardin and C. Peebles (eds), *Representations in archaeology.* University of Indiana Press: Bloomington, IN; 168–77.

—(2007) Appendix E. Ambohimanga: creating a capital and a polity in thought, deed and dirt. In H. Wright, H. (ed.), *Early state formation in central Madagascar: An archaeological survey of western Avaradrano.* Museum of Anthropology, University of Michigan: Ann Arbor, MI; 301–12.

Kus, S. and V. Raharijaona (1998) Between earth and sky there are only a few large boulders: sovereignty and monumentality in Central Madagascar. *JAA* 17: 53–79.

—(2000) House to palace, village to state: scaling up architecture and ideology. *AA* 102(1): 98–113.

—(2001) 'To dare to wear the cloak of another before their very eyes': state co-optation and local re-appropriation in mortuary rituals of Central Madagascar. In M. Chesson (ed.), *Social memory, identity and death: Intradisciplinary perspectives on mortuary rituals.* APAAA 10. John Wiley & Sons: Washington, DC; 114–31.

—(2006) Visible and vocal: sovereigns of the early Merina (Madagascar) state. In T. Inomata and L. Coben (eds), *Archaeology of performance: Theatres of power, community and politics.* Altamira Press: Lanham, MD; 303–29.

Laclau, E. and C. Mouffe (2001) *Hegemony and Socialist Strategy: Towards a Radical Democratic Politics.* 2nd edn. Verso Books: London.

Lapinkivi, P. (2004) *The Sumerian sacred marriage in light of comparative evidence.* State Archives of Assyria Studies 15. The Neo-Assyrian Text Corpus Project: Helsinki.

Larson, P. (2000) *History and Memory in the Age of Enslavement: Becoming Merina in Highland Madagascar, 1770–1822.* Heinemann: Portsmouth, NH.

—(2001) Austronesian mortuary ritual in history: transformation of secondary burial (*Famadihana*) in highland Madagascar. *Ethnohistory* 48(1–2): 123–55.

Latour, B. (2005) *Reassembling the Social: An Introduction to Actor-Network Theory.* Oxford University Press: Oxford.

Law, J. (1992) Notes on the theory of the actor-network: ordering, strategy and heterogeneity. *Systems Practice* 5: 379–93.

Leahy, A. (1995) Ethnic diversity in ancient Egypt. In J. Sasson (ed.), *Civilizations of the Ancient Near East.* Vol. I. Charles Scribner's Sons: New York; 225–34.

Legrain, L. (1936) *Ur Excavations III: Archaic seal impressions.* Trustees of the British Museum and the Museum of the University of Pennsylvania: London.

Lemke, T. (2007) 'An indigestible meal?' Foucault, governmentality and state theory. *Distinktion: Scandinavian Journal of Social Theory* 15: 43–64.

Lenin, V. I. (1976 [1917]) *The State and revolution: The Marxist teaching on the State and the tasks of the proletariat in the revolution.* Foreign Languages Press: Peking.

Leonard, R. and T. Jones (1987) Elements of an inclusive evolutionary model for archaeology. *JAA* 6(3): 199–219.

LeVine, T. (1987) Inka labor service at the regional level: the functional reality. *Ethnohistory* 34(1): 14–46.

LeVine, T. (ed.) (1992) *Inka storage systems.* University of Oaklahoma Press: Norman, OK.

Lévi-Straus, C. (1967) *Structural Anthropology.* Basic Books: Garden City, NY.

Lincoln, B. (1994) *Authority: Construction and Corrosion.* University of Chicago Press: Chicago.

Liu, L. (2009) State emergence in early China. *ARA* 38: 217–32.

Llewellyn-Jones, L. (2007) House and veil in ancient Greece. In R. Westgate, N. Fischer and J. Whitley (eds), *Building Communities: House, Settlement and Society in the Aegean and Beyond. Proceedings of a conference held at Cardiff University, 17–12 April 2001.* British School at Athens: London; 251–8.

Lloyd, G. E. R. (2010) History and human nature: cross-cultural universals and cultural relativities. *Interdisciplinary Science Reviews* 35(3–4): 201–14.

Lloyd, S. (1969) Back to Ingharra: some further thoughts on the excavations at East Kish. *Iraq* 31(1): 40–8.

Lucero, L. (2006) *Water and Rutual: The Rise and Fall of Classic Mayan Rulers.* University of Texas Press: Austin, TX.

Lucero, L. and B. Fash (eds) (2006) *Precolumbian Water Management: Ideology, Ritual and Power.* University of Arizona Press: Tucson, AZ.

Lull, V. and R. Micó (2011) *Archaeology of the origin of the state.* Oxford University Press: Oxford.

McCarthy, T. (1989) Introduction to J. Habermas, *The Structural Transformation of the Public Sphere: An Inquiry into a Category of Bourgeois Society.* Trans. T. Burger. Ploty Press: Cambridge; xi–xiv.

McEwan, G. (2006) *The Incas: New perspectives.* W. W. Norton & Co.: Santa Barbara, CA.

McIntosh, S. (1999) Pathways to complexity: an African perspective. In S. McIntosh (ed.), *Beyond Chiefdoms: Pathways to Complexity in Africa.* Cambridge University Press: Cambridge; 1–30.

Maekawa, K. (1973/74) The development of the E-MI in Lagash during Early Dynastic III. *Mesopotamia* 8–9: 77–144.

Magid, G. (2001) Micromanagement in the é-mi/ᵈBa-ú: notes on the organization of labor at Early Dynastic Lagash. In T. Abusch, P.-A. Beaulieu, J. Huehnergard, P. Machinist, P. Steinkeller (eds), *Historiography in the cuneiform world.* Proceedings of the 45th Rencontre Assyriologique Internationale. Part 1. CDL Press: Bethesda, MD; 313–28.

Mann, M. (1986) *The Sources of Social Power.* Vol. 1. Cambridge University Press: Cambridge.

Marchesi, G. (2004) Who was buried in the Royal Tombs of Ur? The epigraphic and textual data. *Orientalia* 73: 153–97.

Marcus, J. (2008) The archaeological evidence for social evolution. *ARA* 37: 51–66.

Marinetto, M. (2007) *Social theory, the state and modern society: The state in contemporary social thought.* Open University Press: Maidenhead.

Marken, D. (ed.) (2007) *Palenque: Recent Investigations at the Classic Maya Center.* Altamira Press: Lanham, MD.

Mauss, M. (1990) *The Gift: The form and reason for exchange in archaic societies.* Trans. W. Halls. Routledge: New York.

Meskell, L. (2002) *Private life in New Kingdom Egypt.* Princeton University Press: Princeton.

Mitchell, T. (1999) Society, economy, and the state effect. In G. Steinmetz (ed.), *State/Culture: State-Formation after the Cultural Turn.* Cornell University Press: Ithaca, NY; 76–97.

Miyazaki, M. (2007) Public coercive power of the Greek Polis. On a recent debate. *Bulletin of the Institute for Mediterranean Studies, Waseda University* 5: 101–14.

Mizoguchi, K. (2009) Nodes and edges: a network approach to hierarchisation and state formation in Japan. *JAA* 28(1): 14–26.

Molleson, T. and D. Hodgson (1993) A cart driver from Ur. *Archaeozoologia* 6: 93–106.

—(2000) The porters of Ur. *Isimu* 3: 101–18.

—(2003) The human remains from Woolley's excavations at Ur. *Iraq* 65: 91–129.

Monroe, J. C. (2010) Power by design: architecture and politics in precolonial Dahomey. *Journal of Social Archaeology* 10(3): 367–97.

Moore, J. (2006) 'The Indians were much given to their taquis': drumming and generative categories in ancient Andean funerary processions. In T. Inomata and L. Coben (eds), *Archaeology of performance: Theatres of power, community and politics*. Altamira Press: Lanham, MD; 47–79.

Moorey, P. R. S. (1977) What do we know about the people buried in the Royal Cemetery? *Expedition* 20/1: 24–40.

—(1978) *Kish excavations 1923–1933*. Claredon Press: Oxford.

Moortgat, A. (1949) *Tammuz: Der Unsterblichkeitsglaube in der altorientalischen Bildkunst*. DeGruyter: Berlin.

Morera, E. (1990) *Gramsci's historicism: A realist interpretation*. Routledge: London.

Morris, C. and D. E. Thompson (1985) *Huánuco Pampa: An Inca City and its Hinterland*. Thames and Hudson: London.

Morris, I. (2000) *Archaeology as cultural history*. Blackwell: Oxford.

Murra, J. (1962) Cloth and its functions in the Inka state. *AA* 64(4): 710–28.

—(1980) *The economic organization of the Inka state*. JAI Press Inc.: Greenwich, CT.

Nafisi, M. (2004) Class, embeddedness and the modernity of ancient Athens. *CSSH* 46(2): 378–410.

Nagle, D. B. (2006) *The household as the foundation of Aristotle's polis*. Cambridge University Press: Cambridge.

Nevett, L. (1995) Gender relations in the Classical Greek household: the archaeological evidence. *The Annual of the British School at Athens* 90: 363–81.

—(2010a) *Domestic space in classical antiquity*. Key Themes in Ancient History. Cambridge University Press: Cambridge.

—(2010b) Domestic culture in Classical Greece. In O. Hekster and S. Mols (eds), *Cultural Messages in the Graeco-Roman world. Acta of the BABESCH 80th Anniversary Workshop Radboud University Nijmegen, September 8th 2006*. Peeters: Leuven; 49–56.

—(2011) Towards a female topography of the ancient Greek city: case studies from Late Archaic and Early Classical Athens (c.520–400 BCE). *Gender and History* 23(3): 576–96.

O'Brien, M. J., R. L. Lyman, A. Mesoudi and T. L. VanPool (2010) Cultural traits as units of analysis. *Philosophical Transactions of the Royal Society B* 365: 3797–806.

O'Connor, D. (1995) Beloved of Maat, the horizon of Re: the royal palace in New Kingdom Egypt. In D. O'Connor and D. Silverman (eds), *Ancient Egyptian Kingship*. Brill: Leiden; 263–300.

O'Connor, D. and D. Silverman (1995) Introduction to D. O'Connor and D. Silverman (eds), *Ancient Egyptian Kingship*. Brill: Leiden; xvii–xxvii.

Osborne, R. (1997) Law, the democratic citizen and the representation of women in Classical Athens. *Past and Present* 155: 3–33.

Owen, W. F. M. (1833) *Narrative of voyages to explore the shores of Africa, Arabia and Madagascar performed in H.M. ships Leven and Barracouta under command of Capitan W.F.M. Owen by command of the Lord Comminsoners of the Admiralty*. Volume II. Richard Bentley: London.

Parkinson, R. (2002) *Poetry and Culture in Middle Kingdom Egypt: A Dark Side to Perfection*. Equinox Publishing: London.

Pauketat, T. (2007) *Chiefdoms and other archaeological delusions*. Altamira Press: Lanham MD.

Paynter, R. (1989) The archaeology of equality and inequality. *ARA* 18: 369–99.

Peirce, C. (1931) Prolegomena to an apology for Pragmaticism. In C. Hartshorne and P. Weiss (eds), *Collected papers of Charles Sanders Peirce*. Vol. 4. Harvard University Press: Cambridge, MA; 531

Plato (1974) *The Republic*. Trans. G. Grube. Hackett Publishing Co: Indianapolis, IN.

Pluciennik, M. (2005) *Social evolution*. Duckworth: London.

Pollock, S. (1999) *Ancient Mesopotamia: The Eden that never was*. Cambridge University Press: Cambridge.

—(2003) Feast, funerals, and fast food in early Mesopotamian states. In T. Bray (ed.), *The archaeology and politics of feasting in early states and empires*. Kluwer Academic/Plenum Publishers: New York; 17–38.

—(2007a) The Royal Cemetery of Ur: ritual, tradition, and the creation of subjects. In M. Heinz and M. Feldman (eds), *Representations of political Power: Case Histories from Times of Change and Dissolving Order in the Ancient Near East*. Eisenbrauns:Winona Lake, IN; 89–110.

—(2007b) Death of a household. In N. Laneri (ed.), *Performing death: Social analyses of funerary traditions in the ancient Near East and Mediterranean*. Oriental Institute of the University of Chicago: Chicago; 209–22.

Poma de Ayala, F. G. 1936 [1615] *El primer nueva corónica y buen gobierno.*
  Sigio XXI: Institut d'Ethnologie: Paris.
Prentice, R. (2010) *The exchange of goods and services in Pre-Sargonic Lagash.*
  Ugarit-Verlag: Münster.
Prentiss, A., I. Kuijt and J. Chatters (eds) (2009) *Macrevolution in human
  prehistory: Evolutionary theory and processual archaeology.* Springer: New
  York.
Pyburn, K. A. (ed.) (2004) *Ungendering civilization.* Routledge: London.
Raison-Jourde, F. (1991) *Bible et pouvoir à Madagascar au XIXe siècle:
  Invention d'une identité chrétienne et construction de l'État (1780–1880).*
  Éditions Karthala: Paris.
Redman, C. (1978) *The rise of civilization: From early farmers to urban society
  in the ancient Near East.* W. H. Freeman & Co. Ltd: San Francisco.
Renfrew, C. and P. Bahn (2012) *Archaeology: Theories, methods and practice.*
  6th edn. Thames and Hudson: London.
Richards, J. (2000) Modified order, responsive legitimacy, redistributed
  wealth: Egypt 2260–1650 BC. In J. Richards and M. Van Buren (eds),
  Order, legitimacy, and wealth in ancient states. Cambridge University
  Press: Cambridge; 36–45.
Richards, J. and M. Van Buren (eds) (2000) *Order, legitimacy, and wealth in
  ancient states.* Cambridge University Press: Cambridge.
Richerson, P. and R. Boyd (2001) Institutional evolution in the Holocene: the
  rise of complex societies. In W. G. Runciman (ed.), *The origin of human
  social institutions.* Proceedings of the British Academy 110. Published for
  the British Academy by Oxford University Press: Oxford; 197–204.
Robinson, D. M. and J. W. Graham (1938) *Excavations at Olynthus Volume
  8: The hellenic house: A study of the houses found at Olynthus with a
  detailed account of those excavated in 1931 and 1934.* The Johns Hopkins
  University Press: Baltimore.
Rosenberg, J. (1994) *The empire of civil society: A critique of the realist theory
  of International Relations.* Verso Books: London.
Rosenberg, M. (2009) Proximate causation, group selection and the evolution
  of hierarchical human societies: systems, processes and patterns. In A.
  Prentiss, I. Kuijt and J. Chatters (eds), *Macrevolution in human prehistory:
  Evolutionary theory and processual archaeology.* Springer: New York; 23–50.
Routledge, B. (2003) The antiquity of the nation? Critical reflections from the
  ancient Near East. *Nations and Nationalism* 9(2): 213–33.

—(2004) *Moab in the Iron Age: Hegemony, polity archaeology.* University of Pennsylvania Press: Philadelphia.

Sanchez, J. (2005) Ancient Maya royal strategies: creating power and identity through art. *Ancient Mesoamerica* 16: 261–75.

Ste Croix, G. de (1981) *The class struggle in the ancient Greek world: From the Archaic age to the Arab conquest.* Gerald Duckworth & Co. Ltd: London.

Scarborough, V. (1998) Ecology and ritual: Water management and the Maya. *LAA* 9(2): 135–59.

—(2003) *The flow of power: Ancient water systems and landscapes.* SAR Press: Santa Fe, NM.

Scarborough, V. and G. Gallopin (1991) A water storage adaptation in the Maya lowlands. *Science* 251: 658–62.

Schele, L. and M. E. Miller (1986) *The blood of kings: Dynasty and ritual in Maya art.* Thames and Hudson: New York.

Scheidel, W. (1995) The most silent women of Greece and Rome: rural labour and women's life in the ancient world. (I). *Greece and Rome* 42: 202–17.

—(1996) The most silent women of Greece and Rome: rural labour and women's life in the ancient world. (II). *Greece and Rome* 43: 1–10.

Schmandt-Besserat, D. (2001) Feasting in the ancient Near East. In M. Dietler and B. Hayden (eds), *Feasts: Archaeological and ethnographic perspectives on food, politics and power.* Smithsonian Institute Press: Washington, DC; 391–403.

Scott, J. (1985) *Weapons of the weak: Everyday forms of peasant resistance.* Yale University Press: New Haven.

—(1990) *Domination and the arts of resistance.* Yale University Press: New Haven.

—(1998) *Seeing like a State.* Yale University Press: New Haven.

Schwartz, G. (2007) Appendix D. Population and production in eighteenth-century Madagascar: analyzing archaeological evidence of the subsistence economy of the central highlands. In H. Wright (ed.), *Early state formation in central Madagascar: An archaeological survey of western Avaradrano.* Museum of Anthropology, University of Michigan: Ann Arbor, MI; 289–300.

Selz, G. (2004) Early Dynastic vessels in 'ritual' contexts. *Wiener Zeitschrift für die Kundes des Morgenlandes* 94: 185–223.

Seri, A. (2005) *Local power in Old Babylonian Mesopotamia.* Equinox: London.

Shanks, M. (1999) *Art and the early Greek city state: An interpretive archaeology.* Cambridge University Press: Cambridge.

Shanks, M. and C. Tilley (1988) *Social theory and archaeology*. University of New Mexico Press: Albuquerque, NM.

Sibree, J. (1870) *Madagascar and its people. Notes of a four year residence. With a sketch of the history, position and prospects of missionary work amongst the Malagasy*. The Religious Tract Society: London.

Silverblatt, I. (1987) *Moon, sun and witches: Gender ideologies and class in Inca and Colonial Peru*. Princeton University Press: Princeton.

Skinner, Q. (1989) The State. In T. Ball, J. Farr and R. Hanson (eds), *Political innovation and conceptual change*. Cambridge University Press: Cambridge; 90–131.

Smith, A. T. (2003) *The political landscape: Constellations of authority in early complex polities*. University of California Press: Berkeley, CA.

—(2004) The end of the essential archaeological subject. *AD* 11(1): 1–20.

—(2006) Representational aesthetics and political subjectivity: the spectacular in Urartian images of performance. In T. Inomata and L. Coben (eds), *Archaeology of performance: Theatres of power, community and politics*. Altamira Press: Lanham, MD; 103–34.

—(2011) Archaeologies of sovereignty. *ARA* 40: 415–32.

Smith, M. (2005) Networks, territories, and the cartography of ancient states. *Annals of the Association of American Geographers* 95(4): 832–49.

Smith, M. E. and P. Peregrine (2012) Approaches to comparative analysis in archaeology. In M. E. Smith (ed.), *The comparative archaeology of complex societies*. Cambridge University Press: Cambridge; 4–20.

Spencer, C. and E. Redmond (2001) Multilevel selection and political evolution in the Valley of Oaxaca, 500–100 BC *JAA* 20: 195–229.

Stein, G. (1998) Heterogeneity, power, and political economy: some current research issues in the archaeology of Old World complex societies. *Journal of Archaeological Research* 6(1): 1–44.

Steinkeller, P. (1987) The administrative and economic organization of the Ur III state: the core and the periphery. In McG. Gibson and R. Biggs (eds), *The organization of power. Aspects of bureaucracy in the ancient Near East*. The Oriental Institute: Chicago; 19–41.

Stone, A. (1995) *Images from the underworld: Naj Tunich and the tradition of Maya cave painting*. University of Texas Press: Austin, TX.

Surette, F. (2008) *The acllacona: The Inca chosen women in archaeology and history*. Unpublished M.A. dissertation. Trent University.

Taylor, C. (2011) Women's social networks and female friendship in the ancient Greek city. *Gender and History* 23(3): 703–20.

Teeter, E. (1997) *The presentation of Maat: Ritual and legitimacy in ancient Egypt.* Oriental Institute: Chicago.

Tilley, C. (1990) Michel Foucault: Towards an archaeology of archaeology. In C. Tilley (ed.), *Reading material culture.* Blackwell: Oxford; 281–347.

Tilly, C. (1975) Reflections on the history of European state-making. In C. Tilly and G. Ardant (eds), *The formation of national states in Western Europe.* Princeton University Press: Princeton; 3–83.

Tinney, S. (1998) Death and burial in early Mesopotamia: the view from the texts. In Zettler and L. Horne (eds), *Treasures from the Royal Tombs of Ur.* University of Pennsylvania Press: Philadelphia; 26–8.

Turchin, P. (2011) Warfare and the evolution of social complexity: A multilevel-selection approach. *Structure and Dynamics* 4(3): 1–37.

Veni, G. (1990) Maya utilization of karst groundwater resources. *Environmental Geology and Water Sciences* 16: 63–6.

de Veyrières, P. and G. de Méritens (1967) *Le livre de la sagesse malgache: Proverbes, dictons, sentences, expressions figurées et curieuses.* Éditions Maritimes et d'Outre-mer: Paris.

Vidale, M. (2011) PG 1237, Royal Cemetery of Ur: patterns in death. *CAJ* 21(3): 427–51.

Visicato, G. (1995) *The bureaucracy of Šuruppak: Administrative centres, central offices, intermediate structures and hierarchies in the economic documentation of Fara.* Ugarit-Verlag: Münster.

Viveiros de Castro, E. (2004) Perpective anthropology and the method of controlled equivocation. *Tipití* 2(1): 1–20.

van der Vliet, E. (2005) Polis. The problem of statehood. *SEH* 4 (2): 120–50.

Vogel, H. (2008) *Wie man Macht macht: Eine macht- und genderkritische Untersuchung der frühesten Repräsentationen von Staatlichkeit.* Unpublished Ph.D. dissertation, Free University of Berlin.

Vogt, E. (1969) *Zinacantan: A Maya community in the highlands of Chiapas.* Harvard University Press: Cambridge.

Vogt, E. and D. Stuart (2005) Some notes on ritual caves among the ancient and modern Maya. In J. Brady and K. Prufer (eds), *In the maw of the earth monster: Mesoamerican ritual cave use.* University of Texas Press: Austin, TX; 155–85.

Wagner-Hasel, B. (2003) Women's life in Oriental seclusion? On the history and use of a *topos*. In M. Golden and P. Toohey (eds), *Sex and difference in ancient Greece and Rome*. Edinburgh University Press: Edinburgh; 241–52.

Walker, S. (1983) Women and housing in classical Greece. In A. Cameron and A. Kuhrt (eds), *Images of women in Antiquity*. Croom Helm: Beckenham; 81–93.

Weber, J. and R. Zettler (1998) Metal vessels. In R. Zettler and L. Horne (eds), *Treasures from the Royal Tombs of Ur*. University of Pennsylvania Press: Philadelphia; 125–42.

Weber, M. (1978) *Economy and society*. 2 Vols. G. Roth and C. Wittich (eds). University of California Press: Berkeley, CA.

Westgate, R. (2007) The Greek house and the ideology of citizenship. *World Archaeology* 39(2): 229–45.

Westgate, R., N. Fischer and J. Whitley (eds) (2007) *Building Communities: House, Settlement and Society in the Aegean and Beyond. Proceedings of a conference held at Cardiff University, 12–17 April 2001*. British School at Athens: London.

Wernke, S. (2006) The politics of community and Inka statecraft in the Colca Valley, Peru. LAA 17(2): 177–208.

Wetterstrom, W. and H. Wright (2007) Appendix C. A contribution to the paleo-ethnobotany of the central highlands of Madagascar. In H. Wright (ed.), *Early state formation in central Madagascar: An archaeological survey of western Avaradrano*. Museum of Anthropology, University of Michigan Press: Ann Arbor, MI; 281–8.

Wilson, D. S. and E. Sober (1994) Reintroducing group selection to the human behavioral sciences. *Behavioral and Brain Sciences 17*: 585–654.

Winter, I. (2009) Reading ritual in the archaeological record: deposition pattern and function of two artefact types from the Royal Cemetery of Ur. In *On Art in the Ancient Near East*. Collected Essays Vol. 2. Brill: Leiden; pp. 227–70.

Witfogel, K. (1957) *Oriental despotism: A comparative study of total power*. Yale University Press: New Haven.

Wood, E. M. (1988) *Peasant-citizen and slave: The foundations of Athenian democracy*. Verso Books: London.

Woolley, L. (1934) *Ur excavations II: The Royal Cemetery*. Trustees of the British Museum and the Museum of the University of Pennsylvania: London.

—(1955)) *Ur excavations IV: The early periods*. The British Museum: London.

Wright, H. (1977) Recent research on the origin of the state. *ARA* 6: 379–97.

—(ed.) (2007) *Early State Formation in Central Madagascar: An Archaeological Survey of Western Avaradrano*. Museum of Anthropology, University of Michigan: Ann Arbor, MI.

Yoffee, N. (2000) Law courts and the mediation of social conflict in ancient Mesopotamia. In J. Richards and M. Van Buren (eds), *Order, legitimacy, and wealth in ancient states*. Cambridge University Press: Cambridge; 46–63.

—(2005) *Myths of the archaic state: Evolution of the earliest cities, states, and civilizations*. Cambridge University Press: Cambridge.

Zettler, R. (1998) The Royal Cemetery of Ur. In R. Zettler and L. Horne (eds), *Treasures from the Royal Tombs of Ur*. University of Pennsylvania Press: Philadelphia; 21–32.

Zettler, R. and L. Horne (eds) (1998) *Treasures from the Royal Tombs of Ur*. University of Pennsylvania Press: Philadelphia.

Index

Printed in Great Britain
by Amazon

27760624R00117